FREEDOM
OR SLAVERY?

Pat Brooks
Dale Crowley, Jr.
Des Griffin
& the late Haviv Schieber

New Puritan Library

NPL has permission to reprint material from the following sources. Kindly contact them for the full text in each case:

Chapter 1:

William H. Tehan, *Quarterly Comment* (8/89). P.R. Herzig and Company, 71 Broadway, New York, NY 10006.

Myers' Finance and Energy, Watershed Issue (7/11/86), N. 7307 Division, Suite 204, Spokane, WA 99208.

American Banker (7/31/75 & 7/24/89), 1 State Street Plaza, New York, NY 10004.

Chapter 4:

Dale Crowley, P.O. Box 1, Washington, DC 20044. Reprints of radio programs of ''The King's Business'' and article in *Christian News,* Box 168, New Haven, MO 63068.

Chapter 5:

Len Martin, co-author of *Holy Land Betrayed,* with Haviv Schieber. Pro-American Press, P.O. Box 41, Gering, NE 69341. Price of book: $5, plus $1.40 postage.

Chapter 6:

Des Griffin, *Anti-Semitism and the Babylonian Connection.* Emissary Publications, 9205 SE Clackamas Road, Clackamas, OR 97015. Price of book: $5, plus $1.40 shipping.

Library of Congress Catalog Card Number: 90-060334

ISBN: 0-932050-42-5

FOREWORD

Freedom — or Slavery? has been a cooperative effort by several American Christian patriots. All authors have agreed to take no royalties from this work, and all funds received by New Puritan Library for it in excess of its printing and shipping costs will be transferred to New Puritan Life for the leadership and training center described in chapter 7.

Chapters 1, 2, 3, and 7 are my work. The others are by-lined by the particular authors who wrote them: chapter 4 by Dale Crowley, Jr.; chapter 5 by the late Haviv Schieber, with Len Martin; chapter 6 by Des Griffin. Those interested in the work of a particular author are urged to contact him direct and not New Puritan Library. This is a small, family-owned business without clerical help except for occasional volunteers. We regret the fact that we have little time to answer correspondence or engage in philosophical discussions, much as we would like to. Those who have urgent questions are encouraged to phone us at (704) 628-2185. However, we are sometimes away and do not use an answering device in our absence. Try again, if you miss us!

The appendix contains material never before in print all in one place. Appendix A is *The Mayflower Compact* of 1620; B is *The Declaration of Independence* of 1776; C is *The U.S. Constitution;* D is "50 Evidences that the USA is 'Constitutionally Christian' " from the state constitutions of all 50 states; E is Rus Walton's cartoon contrast, "Republic vs. Democracy"; F is the Bible reading schedule my husband and I have used for over 20 years; G is a tract I wrote in the 70s: "A Chain of Prayer." H is the Westminster Confession *Shorter Catechism,* perhaps the best summary of Bible doctrine, "the faith once delivered to the saints" (Jude 3).

Countless acquaintances report that they are "fed up" with the huge volume of unsolicited, photocopied material they receive from patriots. We agree. That is why NPL tries to make distribution of attractive material readily available to all distributors and colporteurs who sense the importance of Hosea 4:6 and Ezekiel 33:1-11.

We urge that readers and prayer warriors subscribe to the publications listed in chapter 7 if you are able to do so. The need for *accurate,* up-to-date information increases daily. We also recommend that readers get books produced by other publishers from Emissary Publications, 9205 SE Clackamas Road, Clackamas, OR 97015. Des Griffin is its manager, and certainly has the finest assortment of books available from a Christian source on the conspiratorial network.

The title question, *Freedom — or Slavery?* may well be answered only by disciplined believers willing to do what God wants done in this hour. Like Esther, you and I have been placed on earth by the Sovereign God in a time of great peril. It is our prayer that every reader of this book will answer God's question through Mordecai to Esther much as she did.

"Who knoweth whether thou art come to the kingdom for such a time as this?"

"Go, gather...fast...I also...will fast likewise; and so will I go in unto the king, which is not according to law; and if I perish, I perish!"

May Almighty God bless and keep you, every one.

Pat Brooks, NPL editor

TABLE OF CONTENTS

Appendix

ECONOMIC DISASTER: GOD'S BIG TEST FOR MANKIND

In this final decade of the 20th Century, we are surely living in the most thrilling days of earth's history. Almighty God is about to humble this whole planet and teach everyone on it just who is King of Kings and Lord of Lords.

Believers worldwide sense the urgency. Many churches, mission, and para-church ministries are working in harmony to get the gospel to all five billion of earth's people.

All of this is being played out against a backdrop of the greatest battle for freedom the world has ever seen. Yet ironies abound. As the Berlin Wall and communism itself crash down in the captive nations, America and the West find ourselves clenched in a totalitarian fist.

Everett Sileven, the pastor in Nebraska who was jailed when his church was padlocked in 1983 for operating an "unregistered" Christian school, found himself indicted as 1990 began. The charge? "Conspiracy to defraud the government"!

On the same absurd charge, a SWAT team descended on the home of Franklin and Susan Sanders, January 9, 1990, at 7:15 A.M. Shoving the seven Sanders children into one room, the government agents in black Ninja uniforms arrested the parents — taking Franklin at once; giving Susan two hours to find a baby sitter.

When the Sanders arrived at jail, they found they were among 26 others all indicted on the same charge, most from their own church. The pastor, Dan Morse, and assistant pastor, Curtis Crenshaw, were also arrested. Morse was accused of "failure to file" with the IRS, despite the fact that he has filed his income tax return every year!

Suddenly Grace Presbyterian Church, a small congregation of the Presbyterian Church in America (PCA), found its pastors, elders, and members considered outlaws in the eyes of the government. Why? What is going on in the land that was once "the land of the free and the home of the brave"?

At issue is just who will rule this planet: Almighty God, or mammon? The Lord Jesus Christ said, "Ye *cannot* serve God and mammon," in Matthew 6:24. That is clearly different from *should not. Cannot* speaks of an impossibility.

Both Sanders and Sileven have been fearless Christian patriots, warning that the debt/money system foisted on America by the financial oligarchy will enslave our land and the whole world. Both have publications. Sileven has *America Today* (P.O. Box 188, Houston, MO 65483); Sanders has *The Moneychanger* (P.O. Box 341753, Memphis, TN 38184). He also wrote *Heiland,* a novel showing America a slave state in 2020. Could enemies want them silenced? Bankrupted by litigation?

It is precisely with the "golden chain" of economic security that Satan most successfully traps the majority in the modern world. Whether it be government (jobs, "entitlements," grants, loans, pensions, benefits — whatever), business (wages, salaries, pensions, bonuses, retirement plans, fringe benefits), or even religious organizations, the net effect is the same.

Still God thunders down the ages that First Commandment: "Thou shalt have no other gods before me." Some years ago I started to think that over, and prayed for understanding. What did it mean, after all?

One day I understood. A person's god is what he looks to to provide for him. Many "go to church" who really look to government, or a company, or even Wall Street

2

to provide for them. If all those sources of economic security were swept away, how many would have faith?

Almighty God is about to bring an economic Fall about as profound as the spiritual Fall in the Garden of Eden. Then we shall find out! Talk is cheap. In the relationship with God, as with all other relationships, *only actions over a period of time show where the heart loyalty is.*

America went on an economic binge during the Reagan era. Many made fortunes during the bull market in stocks and bonds. Many took on huge payments for mortgages in neighborhoods they felt suited them with their government-contract jobs with multinational companies. When the plants shut down, as many already have, perhaps they will find out how others felt who lost their jobs, homes, farms, and businesses earlier.

Reagan was a consummate actor. He attended one of the best evangelical churches on the West Coast before he became President. He even had his pastor, Donn Moonmaw, offer a thoroughly evangelical prayer at his first inauguration, in 1981. But he also attended the occult retreats at Bohemian Grove with the super-rich, and during his White House years neither attended church nor had services there, as the Nixons had.

Finally, it all came out. His wife, Nancy, regularly consulted an astrologer, and in a prime time interview on ABC television during the Fall of 1989, he said, "I am an Aquarian." In other words, he identified himself with the New Age set who are looking for the Aquarian Age to begin, soon!

Reagan liked to be called a "conservative." Yet when he took office in 1981 the federal deficit was just under one trillion dollars; when he left office, it was two-and-a-half times as high. Furthermore, with his incredible "free trade" policies, allowing multinational corporations to close U.S. plants and go overseas for cheap labor without U.S. taxes, he changed America from a credit nation to a debtor nation.

Joseph Sobran, an independent thinker among the editors of *National Review,* recently summed up the pathetic legacy of the "Reagan Revolution" and the New Right: "Part of the problem is that a movement that began in resistance to the welfare state thought it had won a victory when it had only won temporary control of the welfare state apparatus." Most conservatives have "buried their principles," he said, in the "interesting times" in which we live — when socialism and communism are collapsing worldwide. "Is it possible," he concluded, "that the United States will be the last stronghold of collectivism?"[1]

Don Mantooth, a courageous Indiana patriot, has long contended that "the conservative movement has joined the left." He says the New Right Agenda "contains many collectivist objectives. Enterprise zones, public-private partnerships, open borders, free trade, much of the so-called 'economic development,' and many other proposals are pure collectivism."[2]

In terms that believers will understand, looking to the New Right in our present crisis will be "leaning upon Egypt." The army of God will have none within its ranks that deny His Sovereignty or the need of His Salvation through the shed blood of His Son. Both the "New Right" and the "New Agers" are littered with such types.

In order for a people to have the blessing of Almighty God, it must squarely face the implications of Amos 3:3: "Can two walk together, except they be agreed?" The Omnipotent One has no obligation to protect or preserve murderers of the unborn, legalizers of pornography, granters of tax-exempt status to satanist or witchcraft covens, or protectors of money-laundering banks which fund the drug trade.

Quite the contrary. Consistent with His unchanging, righteous character and His many scriptural warnings, He will *destroy* such a society. When He does, only a remnant will be left, no "democratic majority." The 50% plus one in America and the so-called "free world" who think they can outvote God have a surprise coming. It is summarized in Proverbs 2:21 and 23: "For the upright shall dwell in the land, and the perfect shall remain in it. But the wicked shall be cut off from the earth, and the transgressors shall be rooted out of it."

Today America is roughly 95% slave and 5% free. Our freedom resembles that of a frisky terrier in a fenced-in run. Just as the peppy puppy has known nothing but his narrow cage, so most Americans today have known nothing but a humanist "Establishment" which allows prayer and Bible reading in church but not in school; deficit-spending which will enslave our grandchildren and theirs; a media so vile that many now boycott the whole, rather than simply an occasional program.

Yet one can almost hear the questions that arise in the minds of those who hear of that 95% to 5% ratio. "If it is true that we are nearly serfs, to whom or to what are we enslaved?"

Debt. And those who hold the I.O.Us.

"Oh well, that's no problem, for we really 'owe it to ourselves.'"

Sorry about that. Wrong! We owe it to those who own the stock in the 12 private Federal Reserve Banks, never subjected to an outside or government audit since their creation in 1914!

"Really? Why, that's funny. I thought that the Federal Reserve Banks were part of the U.S. Treasury Department. Don't they just work together?"

In a word, no. The whole purpose of the Federal Reserve Act of 1913 was to bypass Article 1, Section 8 of the U.S. Constitution, which gave only *Congress* the right to issue the nation's currency and credit. The big international bankers hated the idea that America could issue her own money, debt free. What they wanted was money *lent* into existence, which they would create and control. This scam

5

required the U.S. Government to *pay them back, with interest,* from then on out. But they knew the debt could never be repaid, for they were very careful *never* to create the money for the interest, only the debt/money principal. That is why, like Pogo, "the hurrier we go, the behinder we get!" U.S. Treasury Bonds represent total economic servitude: running on a treadmill that speeds up every year with bigger and bigger deficits. And, funny thing, the amount the U.S. Federal Budget is in debt every year is usually just about the same as the interest the Federal Reserve is owed: the third largest item on the budget.

"Come on, now. This is hard to believe. Show me some proof that 'the Fed' is not part of the U.S. Government!"

Okay. Go to your library and get a copy of the phone book for Washington, D.C. All U.S. Government listings are on the blue pages. The blue section is sandwiched in between a residential section of white pages and a final business section, also on white pages. There are three listings in that private, business section that relate to our subject: Federal Reserve Bank of New York, Federal Reserve System, and Federal Reserve System Board of Governors.

Yes, the Fed is a private *business,* not a government agency, as these white-page listings make obvious.

Phoebe Courtney comments in her excellent booklet, *Audit the Fed,* that the Federal Reserve Bank of Denver is also listed in the part of that phone book titled "Businesses," rather than in the government section.

She then quotes State Sen. Jack Metcalf from a 1982 speech as follows: "What further proof do we need that the Fed is not an agency of the government than to understand that when the federal government needs more money, the Fed does not merely create and print it as it would do were it a government agency. No, the Fed creates it as a loan and charges the government interest on it."[3]

So much for our "conversation" on the fascinating Fed. NPL will soon release a book by State Senator Jack Metcalf, Dr. Charles Norburn, and V.R. Rossiter, *Fed or Honest Money?* Suffice it to say here that there is finally a move afoot in the Congress to audit the Fed. In the House of Representatives, it is led by Phil Crane (R-IL); in the Senate by Harry Reid (D-NV). Co-sponsors have been coming aboard weekly. Such an audit will remove the veil of secrecy from the Fed that has made its scam possible. The outrage that would follow should produce reform.

Many believers fail to realize that Almighty God abhors both debt and usury. The historic meaning of "usury" in Webster's *Unabridged Dictionary* is simply "interest." It took the semantic muddling of the 20th Century to produce the current meaning of *high* interest. In Ezekiel 18:10-13, scripture equates lending at interest with murder, and promises the death penalty for both.

Man may scoff and smile at these absolute standards, but his trivial attitude will not change God's righteous judgments. Any careful student of God's Word, the Bible, soon realizes that a money system based on debt and usury cannot be blessed of Almighty God. Richard Kelly Hoskins has devoted a fine book to this subject: *War Cycles/Peace Cycles*. He has a monthly investment newsletter, *Portfolios Investment Advisory* (P.O. Box 997, Lynchburg, VA 24505).

Where a money system based on debt and interest has taken us can be seen very quickly in a recent overview of the U.S. National Debt given by Rus Walton, Director of the Plymouth Rock Foundation. "In 1791, just three years after the ratification of the Constitution, the federal debt totalled $75 million. That came to about $18.50 per person...the United States began the 20th Century with a federal debt of $1.2 billion; that came to about $16.60 per capita. At the start of World War I, the debt had climbed to $3 billion [after the passage of the Federal Reserve Act — Ed.]. In 1940, the debt was $51 billion. Just the interest on the debt was $1 billion, equal to the total debt in 1900. By the end of World War II, the debt stood at $256.9 billion ($325 per person)...From 1789 to 1980 the federal government piled up $914 billion in debt. To-day [1988-Ed.] the federal debt is listed as $2.52 trillion; $10,416 per capita.''[4]

As this book is nearing release, it appears that the 1990s will begin with a debt of nearly $3 trillion. Thus, it took 200 years for the national debt to reach its first trillion. That amount has tripled in just one decade.

Clearly, this cannot continue. America and the whole world are facing a disaster of mammoth proportions. Even the best economic minds cannot agree on whether we face inflation or deflation, but most agree on one thing: an economic crash lies ahead.

Late in 1989 economic analyst Don McAlvaney was interviewed by Larry Burkette on the latter's radio program. Burkette asked McAlvaney if he expected recession in 1990, only to be corrected by McAlvaney: ''No, depression,'' he said. He then went on to predict an inflationary depression.

Analysts William H. Tehan, James Dale Davidson, and C.V. Myers disagree, predicting instead devastating *deflation*. Their arguments are so powerful that we present them here.

Tehan quotes the Federal Reserve Bank in St. Louis (6/29/89) as follows, and then gives his own commentary: ''''The M1 money stock declined at a 4.6% annual rate from the four weeks ending December 19, 1988, to the four weeks ending June 19, 1989. A 6-month drop of this magnitude previously has not occurred over the 30-year history of this particular data series.' ...The first major warning of the approaching banking crisis and depression of the 1930s was sounded in 1930 when deposits in all banks in the U.S. contracted from $54.9 billion to $51.8 billion, or by 5.6% in 12 months.

''Since 1980, the U.S. economy has been in a state of dissipating inflation and consolidation after three decades of growth and credit inflation. This consolidation has been characterized by falling commodity prices, declining real estate prices, early retirements in the executive suite, lay-offs at staff and line levels, and closure of plant and equipment."[5]

Incidentally, James Dale Davidson states, "As of July [1989], M1 is down by almost 7% in real terms, a more severe decline than in the equivalent period in 1929."[6]

Davidson also refers to a "silent crash" in real estate. He says, "In spite of falling interest rates, the slump in real estate prices continues to spread. It now affects most markets outside California and the upper Midwest. Total losses approach 1 trillion dollars — greater than the 1987 stock market crash."[7]

C.V. Myers published a "Watershed Issue" of his newsletter in 1986. In it he explained the powerful case for deflation. Here is part of his superb summary:

"There is cash money and there is credit money.

"Cash money is the currency issued by the Federal Reserve. Credit money is the money created by the banks through their lending. When the banks lend $1000, they mark that down as a thousand dollar asset. It becomes credit money. The volume of credit money is governed by this, nothing else. Their assets are their loans.

"The amount of currency in circulation is exceeded 17 or 18 times by the credit money made by the banks. For the Federal Reserve to double the money supply, it would have to issue, print and distribute 17 times as much currency as it has out in the world today...Our system is massively credit money, not cash money....

"We hear a great deal about the growth of the money supply and it's always about M-1. Well, M-1 is a small part of the money supply. It is the money in currency and checking accounts combined. The entire money supply is called M-3 and that includes the currency and the credit money made by the banks.

"So M-3 is the real measure you should watch as far as inflation is concerned because it concerns both CASH money and CREDIT...

"It stands to reason that when the total interest outstrips the total growth of the money supply we have contraction. We are in the process of continuing *contraction*. It is a situation that cannot be remedied by artificial means. The banks cannot create more money because they dare not lend more. In fact, their money supply is shrinking because bad loans are shrinking their assets, as they have to be removed from the books. That means the total money is shrinking. Repayment of loans also shrinks their assets. The banks absolutely cannot flood the money supply — except by making large new loans. But the banks have to suffer the losses on all defaulted loans...

"The exact opposite policies have to be followed to protect oneself against deflation as compared with the policies to protect against inflation.

"The age of protection against inflation passed away during the roaring inflationary 70s when the banks lent like crazy, and gold and silver and all real things rose like crazy.

"This has been followed by the *inevitable* reversal and the unavoidable shrinkage, as the bad debts come to the surface, and shrink the assets.

"As this shrinking goes on, depositor withdrawal takes place, making the situation worse.

"An example is the farm debt. A nationwide shrinkage is taking place here. They estimate that 70% of the 2 1/2 million farms in the U.S. are operating in the red. Nearly half of the family farms are in serious financial trouble. That danger is growing. Of the banks specializing in farm lending, 13% are said to have failed in 1982, 32% in 1984, and nearly twice as many in 1985...

"Therefore , we have an enormous shrinkage in banking assets."[8]

With that background, William Tehan's summary of

the U.S. debt position as we enter the final decade of the 20th Century is hard to refute:

"We think that a 'soft landing' is not possible because the economy is too liquid with debt. In a 'soft landing' the economy lands in a field of expanding credit which cushions the fall. With bank deposits contracting the cushion is missing.

"With economic downturn and falling commodity prices, the third world debt problem is intensifying. Commodity price declines destroy liquidity, capital and loan collateral. Remember oil and Texas, Oklahoma and Colorado.

"Corporate cash flow is slowing precipitously, impairing corporate ability to meet debt obligations...

"Financial problems in the insurance industry are growing. In the past four years, insurance company failure rate has been 250% higher than in the 70s. Since 1987, a dozen life insurance companies have defaulted...

"The economy is slowing rapidly...

"In 1929, the stock market ran up on the same dissipating inflation. A major difference between now and then is that bank deposits were still expanding in the late 1920s. Today, they are contracting. The stock market and the economy are running on a leaking fuel tank."[9]

In a recent conversation with me, William Tehan, author of the above analysis, commented on how tragic will be the outcome of the false expectations of millions. Those who prepare for *inflation* by borrowing home equity loans to finance education, for example, will be wiped out by deflation and may well lose their homes.

Does the Bible speak of a great financial disaster, worse than anything the world has ever experienced before?

Indeed it does. A careful study of Revelation 17 and 18 will show that the primary effect of "Babylon the Harlot" will be economic.

"Alas, alas, that great city Babylon, that mighty city!

For in one hour is thy judgment come. And the merchants of the earth shall weep and mourn over her; for no man buyeth their merchandise any more..."[10]

"For in one hour so great riches is come to nought. And every shipmaster, and all the company in ships, and sailors, and as many as trade by sea, stood afar off, and cried when they saw the smoke of her burning, saying, What city is like this great city!"[11]

What city qualifies for this dubious honor, should it be on earth today? "The City," or financial district of London, where the price of gold is set every day in the Bank of England? New York, where Wall Street and the Federal Reserve Bank have used the debt/usury system to bankrupt America, turning the once-free U.S. Government into a puppet through which its hand exerts its will?

Or could it be Tokyo, where the greatest transfer of wealth in the history of the world has taken place since the Trilateral Commission was formed in 1973? It is worthy of note that this front organization for the goals of its founders, David Rockefeller and a shadowy few of the financial elite, state their *official* purpose as follows, in each issue of their quarterly *Trialogue:*

"The Trilateral Commission was formed in 1973 by private citizens of Western Europe, Japan and North America to foster closer cooperation between these three regions on common problems. It seeks to improve public understanding of such problems, to support proposals to handle them jointly, and to nurture habits and practices of working together among these regions."

Yet, if history has taught us anything, we must learn to watch what financiers do, not what they say. In that light, is "cooperation" the right word to describe what has happened, or *plunder?*

Sometimes one picture is worth a thousand words. The two charts that follow tell the whole story. These are lists

World Rank 12/31/74	(Exclusive of Mutual Savings Banks)		Deposits in U.S. Dollars(a) 12/31/74(b) (,000)
1	Bank of America NT&SA, San Francisco	United States	51,192,118
2	First National City Bank, New York	United States	44,989,342
3	Chase Manhattan Bank NA, New York	United States	34,521,401
4	Banque Nationale de Paris	France	34,229,651†
5	Deutsche Bank, Frankfurt	Germany	30,436,986†
6	Barclays Bank, Ltd., London	England	29,263,190†
7	National Westminster Bank, Ltd., London	England	28,900,231†
8	Credit Lyonnais, Paris	France	28,500,470†
9	Societe Generale, Paris	France	27,239,458†
10	Dresdner Bank, Frankfurt	Germany	24,062,945†
11	Dai-Ichi Kangyo Bank, Ltd., Tokyo	Japan	23,045,859*
12	Westdeutsche Landesbank Girozentrale, Duesseldorf	Germany	22,301,422*
13	Manufacturers Hanover Trust Co., New York	United States	21,248,889
14	Midland Bank, Ltd., London	England	21,208,348†
15	Royal Bank of Canada, Montreal	Canada	20,646,397†
16	Sumitomo Bank, Ltd., Osaka	Japan	20,358,845†
17	Fuji Bank, Ltd., Tokyo	Japan	20,180,854†
18	Morgan Guaranty Trust Co., New York	United States	19,792,224
19	Lloyds Bank, Ltd., London	England	19,248,467†
20	Mitsubishi Bank, Ltd., Tokyo	Japan	19,058,244†
21	Canadian Imperial Bank of Commerce, Toronto	Canada	18,757,513†
22	Industrial Bank of Japan, Ltd., Tokyo	Japan	18,135,893*
23	Sanwa Bank, Ltd., Osaka	Japan	18,073,692†
24	Banca Nazionale del Lavoro, Rome	Italy	17,907,339†
25	Banca Commerciale Italiana, Milan	Italy	17,701,484†
26	Chemical Bank, New York	United States	17,641,943
27	Commerzbank, Duesseldorf	Germany	17,337,659†
28	Bank of Montreal	Canada	16,900,288†
29	Bankers Trust Co., New York	United States	16,175,917
30	Bayerische Vereinsbank, Munich	Germany	16,157,527†

12

Rank 12/88			Deposits 12/31/88 (U.S. Dollars)
1	Dai-Ichi Kangyo Bank Ltd., Tokyo	Japan	312,465,781,696s
2	Sumitomo Bank Ltd., Osaka	Japan	296,000,827,700s
3	Fuji Bank, Ltd., Tokyo	Japan	283,585,351,200s
4	Mitsubishi Bank Ltd., Tokyo	Japan	269,427,020,100u
5	Sanwa Bank Ltd., Osaka	Japan	269,032,279,492s
6	Industrial Bank of Japan, Ltd., Tokyo	Japan	215,397,605,132u
7	Norinchukin Bank, Tokyo	Japan	210,759,455,544
8	Mitsubishi Trust & Banking Corp., Tokyo	Japan	185,955,516,200u
9	Sumitomo Trust & Banking Co., Ltd., Osaka	Japan	177,932,182,096u
10	Tokai Bank Ltd., Nagoya	Japan	175,600,895,540s
11	Mitsui Trust & Banking Co., Ltd., Tokyo	Japan	161,228,496,316
12	Mitsui Bank, Ltd., Tokyo	Japan	159,039,606,488s
13	Banque Nationale de Paris	France	158,549,122,000s
14	Barclays Bank Plc, London	United Kingdom	157,357,472,000s
15	Deutsche Bank, Frankfurt	Germany	154,974,576,400s
16	National Westminster Bank Plc, London	United Kingdom	153,645,648,000s
17	Credit Lyonnais, Paris	France	148,842,971,595s
18	Long-Term Credit Bank of Japan Ltd., Tokyo	Japan	147,426,607,488u
19	Credit Agricole Mutuel, Paris	France	141,973,000,000u
20	Taiyo Kobe Bank, Ltd., Kobe	Japan	138,986,023,792u
21	Daiwa Bank, Ltd., Osaka	Japan	134,466,778,400u
22	Bank of Tokyo, Ltd.	Japan	132,147,474,612u
23	Yasuda Trust & Banking Co. Ltd., Tokyo	Japan	131,788,381,988
24	Societe Generale, Paris	France	123,187,087,000s
25	Dresdner Bank, Frankfurt	Germany	120,317,120,000s
26	Toyo Trust & Banking Co. Ltd., Tokyo	Japan	105,384,007,332
27	Citibank NA, New York	United States	104,996,000,000
28	Hongkong and Shanghai Banking Corp., Hong Kong	Hong Kong	101,841,280,000s
29	Nippon Credit Bank, Ltd., Tokyo	Japan	96,733,830,308
30	Commerzbank, Frankfurt	Germany	94,904,206,676s

13

of the 30 largest banks in the world, rated by their value in billions of dollars of deposits. The first is the list for 1974, just after the Trilateral Commission was formed; the second for 1989, 15 years later.

Please note that the 1974 report showed seven U.S. banks among the top 30 and six Japanese banks. The 1989 report showed one U.S. bank, Citicorp, as #27 on the list, with 19 Japanese banks. Note the top 12 banks in the world are now in Japan.

Is there any greater transfer of wealth in recorded history? The record shows clearly that Japan, which lost the hot war of the 1940s, has won the trade war, courtesy of David Rockefeller's "Trilateral Commission."

Pearl Harbor II, a 30-page report by Robert A. Czeschin, tells how it happened. After China fell to communism (courtesy of the U.S. State Department) and the Korean War, America needed an "ally" in the Far East.

Enter U.S. Ambassador Joseph Dodge (Detroit banker) to Japan in 1949, replacing deindustrializer Edwin Pauley. "The Dodge Line" devalued the yen, launching the deflationary export hemorrhage soon to follow.

Target? America. Goal? Japanese trade surpluses that boggle the mind. Czeschin states, "The first wave of direct Japanese investment came when the big Japanese automakers — Nissan, Honda, Mazda, Mitsubishi, and Toyota — built assembly plants in the Midwest...Tennessee Governor Lamar Alexander, for example, announced his goal was to 'get the Tennessee economy integrated with the Japanese economy.' ...Japanese investment in U.S. real estate rose from $.6 billion in 1984 to $1.2 in 1985 and $5.5 billion in 1986."[14]

By 1989, that figure had climbed so fast, according to columnist Jack Anderson, that the Japanese own $9 billion in Hawaii, alone. Japanese millionaires have driven up real estate prices by 50% since 1987. " 'They are buying up our homes and our farmlands,' laments Honolulu's Mayor

Frank Fasi. 'Many Hawaiians can no longer afford to live here.' ''[15]

The same article gave U.S. Commerce Department figures of total foreign investment in America as $1.5 trillion, roughly one-half the size of the U.S. National Debt!

Where are foreign nations putting their money? According to Anderson, 20% of all U.S. bank assets are now foreign-owned, as well as 64% of Los Angeles real estate, and 39% of Houston real estate. Some 3 million Americans now work for foreign-controlled companies. The Japanese alone have 155 firms here and spend $50 million a year paying lobbyists to further their interests in Washington, D.C.[16]

But most ominous of all, Japanese investors finance 40% of the U.S. federal deficit. Where would America get the money to pay interest on Federal Reserve debt-money if interest rates would drop so low that Japan, Saudi Arabia, Great Britain, and the Netherlands no longer care to buy U.S. Treasury Bonds?

Come to think of it, has *foreclosure* been the goal all along?

CHAPTER TWO

BETRAYAL: SYMPTOM OF APOSTASY

Daniel Burstein, author of *Yen,* spent an evening with host Masaaki Kurokawa, head of Japan's Normura Securities International, a company 20 times the size of Merrill Lynch. Kurokawa spoke of America's huge debt, how Japan had become the world's largest creditor, and America had sunk to the position of the world's greatest debtor: even worse than Argentina and Brazil.

Then Kurokawa gave his plan to "help" the situation. "A single joint currency would be created, dollar on one side, yen on the other," said the Japanese tycoon. He then went on to explain how this would wipe out Japan's currency advantage over America overnight, strengthening American domestic industries against Japanese imports.

How considerate! And just what would Japan like in return?

"California," Kurokawa said.[1]

Unfortunately, this was not meant to be a joke. An advisor of former Japanese Prime Minister Nakasone suggested buying Hawaii outright as a way of settling American trade deficits with Japan.[2]

Nor are the Japanese the only ones to think of debt-for-equity swaps. The World Conservation Bank (WCB) was founded at the fourth World Wilderness Congress held September 11-13, 1987, at Denver, and from the 14th to the 18th at the Aspen Institute for Humanistic Studies at Estes Park, Colorado. An official host of the conference

17

was George W. Hunt, interviewed by outstanding Christian patriot Franklin Sanders in his February, 1988, *Moneychanger* (P.O. Box 341753, Memphis, TN 38184).

Hunt, an accountant for small businesses, corporations, and partnerships, was remarkably candid about the conference. He said the conference was "billed as a worldwide meeting to address global environmental concerns," supposedly produced by wealthy British industrialist Ian Player. However, Hunt claimed he realized later, the real backers of the conference were "the moneychangers in London and Europe...Baron Edmund de Rothschild was at the meeting for six days...personally conducting the monetary matters and creation of this World Conservation Bank (WCB), in the company of I. Michael Sweatman of the Royal Bank of Canada. These two were like Siamese twins, and that's why it appears they were running at least the money side of the conference...primarily to get money. Also, David Rockefeller (of Chase Manhattan Bank) was there, and gave a speech on Sunday.

"The thing that really set me off was Secretary of Treasury James Baker's speech [Note: Baker is the Bush Administration Secretary of State - Ed.]... He gave the keynote address. He said that conservation requires 'growth and development.' There was a HUM around the audience, because they knew that 'growth and development' are antagonistic to conservation...He's talking in code about the *formula,* the 'equation' of conservation and growth and development, that is, assets equals liabilities plus net worth. There were a lot of these double *entendres....*

"They're planning on refinancing, debt-swapping (for assets) $1 trillion of Third World debt into this new WCB....The WCB will be enacted by the United Nations, and will need to be approved, I would think, by every country participating. Let's assume that our senators and congressmen allow this thing to happen. *Then the Bank will be endowed with 30% of the earth's land surface* [Italics added]."[3]

Now, before anyone has apoplexy at the idea of the international bankers having de facto ownership of nearly one-third of the earth's land surface, let us face some facts about America. For years it has been known that the U.S. Government owns one-third of the land mass of the United States. In fact, in recent years one way which has been promoted to end the national debt is the selling off of many such lands and buildings to private buyers.

However, in the light of foreign interests gobbling up American assets right now to use their billions of excess dollars generated by suicidal U.S. trade deficits, is this wise? Even more to the point, should those who hold stock in the twelve Federal Reserve Banks ever decide to foreclose on the United States, just who would get the lion's share?

This is an unsettling topic. The owners of the Fed stock have never been disclosed to Congress or any official agency of the U.S. Government. Just as the Fed has never been audited, so have its owners chosen complete anonymity. Rumors persist that over 50 % of the ownership of the stock lies with European, primarily House of Rothschild banking interests. What does this mean, if true?

For starters, it may mean that America is no longer a sovereign nation, in charge of its own destiny, under God. Remember that dog in the fenced-in run so high that he could never escape? Yes, he is fed and patted occasionally. Yes, he is told soothing ''nothings'' by his masters. Of course he is sometimes called outside his cage to guard the house or fight some current enemy of his masters. He may lose his life in that exercise, alas! But not to worry. There are always plenty more of his kind to send out in the next wave.

Exaggeration? Consider. In both the Korean and Vietnam Wars, American men fought, not under an American flag, but a United Nations flag. Furthermore, this was more than a mere ''insult'' to Old Glory and our men who fought and died and were captured on the other side of the world.

Ever since the UN was founded in 1945 it has served as an organ of official treason and betrayal of America and the so-called Free World. The Rockefeller family gave the land for its Tower of Babel to be built upon in New York City. Red traitors Alger Hiss and Harry Dexter White were the bureaucrats within the Executive Branch of the U.S. Government who guided the whole process to fulfillment. And the U.S. State Department, as well as many in Congress, have acted ever since as if the U.S. Constitution is already suspended, American sovereignty is null and void, and the ''New World Order'' is an established fact.

Furthermore, the commander of the UN military forces has always been a Red. The UN Under-Secretary for Political and Security Affairs has been an official of the USSR, with no exceptions, since 1945!

In practical terms, this has meant that American and other Free-World military men have been subjected to that total control of their Red enemies every time they met them in conflict. The real miracle is that they won any battles at all, under such treachery.

General Lewis Walt wrote a powerful book describing what this meant in the Korean War. *The Eleventh Hour* could have been a bestseller had it been allowed distribution in major book stores and libraries, but the mysterious hand of secret censorship removed it from the shelves soon after its appearance. Here is General Walt's analysis of his predicament from this great book, now out of print:

''It bothered me deeply that I was required to submit 24 hours in advance a detailed plan of attack for approval by UN command headquarters. It bothered me because it soon became apparent that each time we attacked, the enemy was waiting for us. Only by supreme effort and teamwork on the part of my Marines were we able to win our objective and defeat the local enemy forces.

''We were literally in a *Catch 22* situation. We could not achieve surprise. We could not retain anything we won.

But we could not afford not to attack, for if we had not, the Chinese would have been able to build up their forces to overwhelming numbers which could then have broken through our lines and annihilated our forces. We had to keep them off balance. *The Chinese fought under no UN restrictions* [Italics added]."[4]

No wonder the emotional and spiritual scars of both Korea and Vietnam are so deep. The *1989 Information Please Almanac* lists 54,246 American dead from the Korean War; 58,135 American dead from what it calls "The War in Southeast Asia." In addition, thousands were never accounted for in both wars: *the POWs (prisoners of war) and MIAs (missing in action) of which there have been so many reports of live sightings in both areas in recent years.*

Chuck Dean has written a powerful recent book, *Nam Vet,* about his experience during and after the Vietnam War. He confirms what General Walt wrote of the Korean conflict, but from the viewpoint of a paratrooper-called-to-be-cannon-fodder, rather than an officer sending such men into the field. Here is some of what he wrote:

"It became clear to us (while still in combat or upon arriving home) that our country and commanders had betrayed us. We felt lied to about the purpose of most of the things we were ordered to do...

"Probably the single most devastating thing for us was the 'scapegoating' that this country heaped upon the Vietnam returnee. Not only did we come home with a good case of survivor's guilt (feelings of guilt because we had survived combat while close friends did not), but student activists, the press and a lot of churches generated a moral guilt...[5]

"The average age of the World War II soldier was 24. For Americans in Vietnam it was 18. It was the first teenage war ever fought...[6]

"Of those veterans who were married before going to Vietnam, 38% were divorced within six months of returning from Southeast Asia.

"The divorce rate for all Vietnam veterans is in the 90th percentile.

"The suicide rate among veterans *who have completed the local VA program* is estimated at 2.5 per hundred. The national accidental death and suicide rate is 14,000 men per year, 33% above the national average.

"50,000 plus died in the Vietnam War. 70,000 have committed suicide since the war ended.

"500,000 Vietnam veterans have been arrested or incarcerated by the law. It is estimated that there are 100,000 Vietnam vets in prison today and 200,000 on parole.

"Drug and alcohol abuse problems range between 50% to 75%.

"40% are unemployed and 25% earn less than $7,000 per year."[7]

Chuck Dean and a growing number of his buddies have found an answer to their turmoil and bitterness, but not in any government program. He found peace and purpose through faith in the Lord Jesus Christ. "I was now what I had always told myself I would never be: a Christian. But I now understood that a Christian is a person remade by God into a new, eternal, joyous being. I knew whatever happened now, it would be all right. I would be all right. This calming secure sensibility replaced the feelings of death, fear and agony that I had experienced and expected to experience for the rest of my life."[8]

Chuck Dean went on to found "Point Man International" (address in footnotes) to help other Vietnam vets afflicted with Post-Traumatic Stress Disorder (PTSD) which he claims all of them have. There are chapters of the organization in many states, Canada, and New Zealand.

Before we go further, it is time to take stock. What do Japanese or Rothschild-sponsored "debt-for-equity" swaps have in common with no-win wars fought under a UN flag?

A one-word answer tells it all. *Betrayal.* It is the earmark of a selfish, cynical, sullen age. The Lord Jesus Christ said that such a time would come, in His Olivet discourse.

"And then shall *many* be offended, and shall betray one another, and shall hate one another. And *many* false prophets shall arise, and shall deceive *many*. And because iniquity shall abound, the love of *many* shall wax cold. But he that shall endure to the end, the same shall be saved. And this gospel of the kingdom shall be preached in all the world for a witness unto all nations; and then shall the end come."[9]

Many betray, and many deceive many — not a small problem. Furthermore, with the great increase in iniquity, *many* lose their love for God and fellow believers. But, praise God, the persevering saints will endure to the end! Obviously, these are the ones who will preach the "gospel of the kingdom in all the world."

Strange to say, it is "kingdom theology" that is receiving the worst press in many Christian circles today. Yet those who warn of error lump everything from "name-it-and-claim-it," word-faith hedonism to paramilitary white supremacists under "kingdom theology"! And many have the gall to include in the mish-mash the most solid Christian Reconstructionists on this planet: the Covenant, Reformed Theology believers who regard "Thy kingdom come, thy will be done, in earth as it is in heaven" as imperative on their lives.

Who is doing the warning? Almost without exception, the fingerpointers are Dispensationalists who have convinced themselves that the Reconstructionists no longer believe that the Lord Jesus Christ will return.

As a Reconstructionist myself, I can assure you that that is nonsense. We look for the Lord's Return as our blessed hope just as they do, but with one important difference. We do not believe there will ever be any "Pre-Tribulation Rapture" (or catching up) of the saints. No, that whole notion is pure Dispensationalism, just as "Christian Zionism" is. Perhaps some defining of terms is in order here.

In Bible-believing Christianity today there are three major camps. Oddly enough, they are most clearly categorized by their teaching on Israel. The Dispensational group (perhaps 90% of American Fundamentalist and Pentecostal circles) say the Jews are Israel. Covenant, Reformed theology doctrine (roughly 5% of American evangelicals) says the church is Israel. Identity movement adherents say the Anglo-Saxon and related Western peoples are Israel. (The latter include another 5% of evangelicals, plus perhaps an equal number of people who are not born-again Christians at all. More of that later.)

Let me say at the outset that this author is no theologian, only an investigative reporter in such matters. My comments are not to be taken as anything more than what I have observed in Christian circles over the years.

Few theologians want to tackle this task! Perhaps it is the fear of alienating so many who will disagree, within the Christian community. At any rate, I pray that these pages will be taken the way they are offered: in Christian love, with real appreciation for regenerated believers in all camps.

Since Dispensationalism is largest, with the sheer force of numbers, we shall take a close look there, first. The name of the doctrine comes from a view that God judges men differently in each of several dispensations, or periods of time. Moderate Dispensationalists may have only three such periods; ultra-Dispensationalists usually have seven. (These are listed in *Unger's Bible Dictionary.*)

The fountainhead for Dispensational teaching in America is Dallas Theological Seminary in Texas, with Grace Theological Seminary in Indiana, Moody Bible Institute in Chicago, and Biola in the Los Angeles area plus hundreds of other schools in essential agreement.

Two views appear to be shared by most Dispensationalists: the idea that the Jews are Israel, and that the current Israeli state is the fulfillment of Biblical prophecy, which may be summarized as "Christian Zionism"; and the theory that the church (i.e., the sum total of all born-again believers) will be "raptured" (i.e., caught up to be with the Lord Jesus) either just before the Great Tribulation here on earth, or possibly, in the middle of it. Both of these views require a "futurist" interpretation of the Book of Revelation, the Apocalypse. In other words, Dispensationalists see most of Revelation as end-time prophecy, rather than a panoramic view of the Christian era.

Covenant, Reformed Theology (i.e., that which was born in the Reformation) is far more likely to take the "historicist" approach to Revelation: that which emphasizes God's sovereign hand in the affairs of men over the ages, rather than a preoccupation with eschatology, or end-time events culminating in the Return of Jesus Christ. Reformed theology developed from the systematizing John Calvin of Geneva, Switzerland (1509-64) gave to Bible doctrine. It led to the Presbyterian and Puritan movements in the British Isles; the Reformed movement in the Netherlands and on the continent of Europe. The greatest summary of Reformed doctrine is the Westminster Confession of Faith, hammered out by 1100 Puritan and Presbyterian scholars in 1643, fully accepted by their counterparts in America.[10] (See Appendix H for its *Shorter Catechism.*)

This author shares the view that the Westminster Confession of Faith and its Shorter Catechism provide the finest summary of Biblical Christianity ever written. Every professing Christian should read it at least once in a lifetime. Seminaries based on Reform doctrine are Westminster in Philadelphia; Reformed in Jackson, Mississippi; and Covenant in St. Louis. Adherence to the Westminster Confession is widely believed in Reformed circles to be identical to contending "for the faith once delivered to the saints." Departure from it is regarded as apostasy, and several large denominations have taken such a tragic stand.

Reformed Theology says the church is Israel: that the fulfillment of Genesis 12:3, God's covenant with Abraham, is fulfilled in Christ and His redeemed. Old Testament saints were saved looking forward to Calvary and the Resurrection of Jesus Christ; New Testament saints are saved looking back to the same atonement. Such chapters of scripture as Romans 4 and Galatians 3 fully support this view.

The Kingdom/Identity movement says the Anglo-Saxon and related Western people are Israel. It has no seminaries of which this author is aware. (Please correct me if I am wrong!) Its teachers and adherents are largely those which were trained in the two systems already mentioned, but who are concerned that archaeological and historical tracings of the migration of the so-called "Lost Tribes" of Israel have been ignored by the other two.

"British Israelism," as the Kingdom/Identity movement is sometimes called, stresses that God divided the Children of Israel into two kingdoms, two houses, in the time of King Rehoboam, grandson of King David. This event occurred in I Kings 12. From that time to the end of the Old Testament a strong case can be made that the Almighty never equated the House of Israel with the House of Judah, although Ezekiel 37:15-20 prophesied their joining at some future time.

The House of Israel was conquered and removed from their northern kingdom in 722 B.C. by the Assyrians. This event is recorded in history and in the Bible in II Kings 18:9-12. Eight years later the Assyrian King Sennacherib also took captive all the fenced cities of the southern kingdom of Judah (46 of them according to cuneiform records), recorded in verse 13 of the same passage just mentioned. Thus, the House of Judah, left only in Jerusalem, was a much smaller remnant. This group was also given over to divine judgment for their apostasy, as Israel had been. The Babylonian Captivity of 586 B.C. took less than 50,000 of the House of Judah to Babylon for 70 years, as prophesied in Jeremiah 24:8-11.

The word translated "Jew" in our English Bibles first appears in II Kings 16:6 in reference to Syrian raids, before the Assyrian Captivity. The Hebrew word so translated is *Yehudim,* which means "of Judah." The House of Judah included the tribes Judah, Benjamin, and some of Levi (the priestly tribe scattered among all tribes, for they had no land inheritance of their own). The New Testament word "Jew" is the Greek *Ioudaioi* which means *Judeans.* In other words, it has more to do with geography than ancestry, a point which Identity groups stress. History does show that the Edomites or Idumeans (descendants of Esau) were required to become Jews in the time of the Maccabeans.

Identity folks make much of the latter facts, stressing that the Lord Jesus Christ was denoting such non-ethnic Jews in John 8:44. However, the context clearly reveals that the division point between blessed and cursed in John 8 is identical to that of the aforementioned passages in Romans 4 and Galatians 3. Believers in Christ are blessed in Him; those who refuse to believe Him are under a divine curse, since God has provided no other way of salvation (John 14:6 and Acts 4:12).

It is precisely on the point of ethnic salvation that this author parts company with both the Dispensationalists and the Identity folks! Sad to say, although both groups have an intense dislike for one another, they share a very similar view which cannot be supported by any of the Scriptures of the last paragraph. Dispensationalists often believe that God has some other way to save the Jews than through faith in the shed blood of Jesus Christ and His Resurrection. So do some Identity people believe that God will save the Western peoples whether they are born-again through faith in Christ or not. (In all fairness, the evangelicals among them hold out no such false hope.)

The Apostle Paul made it clear in his letter to the Galatians that *no one,* not even he, or an angel from heaven, can pervert the gospel of salvation in Jesus Christ and get away with it (Galatians 1:1-12). That is why I am a Reformed, Covenant Theology believer, regardless of how much I appreciate some contributions from the other two camps.

It is well to note that many Dispensationalists are effective in evangelism and grounding believers in the basics of Christian doctrine. They sometimes raise far more for missions, per capita, than those in either of the other two camps. The Great Commission is the last command of the Lord Jesus Christ, and is recorded in all four gospels. Therefore, it is not to be taken lightly, nor is it to be ignored or considered fulfilled until the Lord Jesus Christ comes back. Thank God for effective witnesses for Christ among the Dispensationalists!

In the same way, I personally have been blessed by research into the migrations of the House of Israel and the very powerful evidence that we Western peoples are indeed their descendants. The fact that heretics like the late Herbert W. Armstrong also stumbled on that truth does not change it any more than his belief that 2 X 2 = 4 could change arithmetic! It is impossible for me to discuss that subject in detail here, but it is covered in two chapters of my former book, *Hear, O Israel,* reprinted in *The Budding Fig Tree,* published by NPL.

Suffice it to say that the knowledge of *who we are* has served to show me just another proof of how powerful our sovereign God is. He has reached the people He said He would reach with the gospel, and He has used the 12 tribes to get it to the rest of the people of the earth. Emphatically, there will be some from every tribe and tongue and nation in the company of the redeemed! (Revelation 7:9.) There is no racial or color barrier keeping anyone from

Christ: only their own hardened hearts. Whosoever will may come. (See the glorious invitation at the very end of the Bible, in Revelation 22:17.)

In summary, God deals with His people according to His standards, not ours. There is a relationship between apostasy, betrayal, and treason. Departing from Almighty God invites His judgment. The terrible apostasy which has taken place in recent decades may well bring awesome judgments. Deuteronomy 28 is still in the Book, whether Dispensationalists ignore it as "not for today" or not.

In that context, the recent transfer of wealth from America to Japan must be seen as more than the machinations of the financial oligarchy through the Trilateral Commission! As Job said, "The LORD gave, and the LORD hath taken away; blessed be the name of the LORD."

Not until Americans begin to realize that our country's greatness lay in her strong foundation of Covenant Theology, "the faith once delivered to the saints," with a *return* to that faith, are things going to change.

It is not some odd, historical trivia that 65-70% of early Americans believed that way. Nor is it a matter of indifference that only 5% now do.

Meanwhile, as America's Christians fight among themselves and strain at gnats as they swallow camels, she teeters at the edge of the abyss. Will America survive? Even more to the point, *should* she?

Let us take a look at her roots and find out.

CHAPTER THREE

IS AMERICA A CHRISTIAN NATION?

What's in a name?

Some years back Dr. Charles W. Ewing sent us an un-published manuscript with the following etymology on the word "America."

"We were all taught in school that this great continent was named after the geographer, Amerigo Vespucci, but we were not taught the meaning of this man's first name.

"Professor Miskovsky, scientist in Etymology at Ob-erlin College, Oberlin, Ohio, brought up some astonish-ing facts about the word 'America.' The Latin form of *'Amerigo'* is *'Americus,'* and the feminine form of *'Americus'* is *'America.'*

"The old Gothic form...for the word *'America'* was *'Amel Ric.'* *Amel Ric* is still found in the German language in a slightly corrupted form as *'Emerich.'*...*Amel* means 'Heaven' and Ric means 'Kingdom.' Together the words mean 'Kingdom of Heaven'..."

Multitudes of believers use the Lord's Prayer faithfully. Every time we repeat the words, "Thy kingdom come; thy will be done on earth, as it is in heaven," we affirm the absolute sovereignty of Almighty God. We are not only declaring His absolute right to rule, but also our agree-ment with His purpose to establish His kingdom.

The early Christians understood that. When the 41 heads of families on the *Mayflower* dedicated their colony "for the glory of God and the advancement of the Christian Faith," they were laying the cornerstone for America. Their Mayflower Compact of 1620 is Appendix A of this book. Later came *A Model for Christian Charity,* the Puritan covenant written by Governor John Winthrop on the *Arbella.* The Massachusetts Bay Colony soon became known as "The Bible State," a theocracy which provided leadership and a scriptural example for the other colonies and the states which were to come, along with the Plymouth Colony of the Pilgrim Separatists.

Today there is a war between good and evil in America, between Christianity and humanism, that dwarfs all other issues. Many refuse to acknowledge that America was founded as a Christian republic, not a "pluralistic democracy."

Sen. Howard Metzenbaum (D-OH) gave an ominous illustration of this challenge in his campaign for re-election in 1988. Addressing a Jewish audience at the Wise Center in Cincinnati, he warned that his hearers should not allow "the forces of evil to make America a Christian nation"! George Voinovich, his Republican opponent, tried to publicize this statement, to no avail. The major news media and the national Republican Party saw to it that the story was spiked. We read of it in Lawrence Patterson's *Monthly Lesson in Criminal Politics* (11/88) and Don Wildmon's *American Family Association Journal* (12/88).

The election outcome? Metzenbaum won with 52% of the vote over the 48% that Voinovich received.

It is high time American Christians go back to their roots. Has no one noticed that it is all right for Israel to be a Jewish nation, and Saudi Arabia to be a Muslim nation, but *unthinkable* for America to be a Christian nation? How long will Christians agree with such dangerous propaganda and disinformation? How long will we pray or sing "God bless America" if we ignore God's hand and rebel against His purpose for her? Put another way, if the Almighty has chosen America to be the headquarters for

His kingdom and get the gospel to the farthest corners of the earth from here, who is prepared to fight against *Him,* and still expect to prosper? (Job 9:4)

The Plymouth Rock Foundation, founded by John and Rosalin Talcott and directed by Rus Walton, is doing a great job of rediscovering our Christian heritage. It is also publishing position papers reflecting scriptural principles on issues of our day called a FAC-Sheet. The "FAC" stands for *Fundamentals for American Christians,* the basic Bible course by Rus Walton undergirding this work. Most recently the Plymouth Rock folks have started "COMCORS" groups, named for the early "Committees of Correspondence" Samuel Adams used so effectively to inform and motivate colonial Christians just before America's War for Independence. (See Plymouth Rock Foundation's cartoon charts contrasting a republic with a democracy in the Appendix at the back of this book.)

In 1988 a lady wrote Justice Sandra O'Connor asking if the Supreme Court has ever declared America to be a Christian nation. The letter she got in answer is reprinted here.

The late Justice David J. Brewer gave an address at Harvard in 1905 documenting that America is a Christian nation. He referred to Supreme Court cases, both state and federal, and many state documents and constitutions. In summary he said: "In no charter or constitution is there anything to even suggest that any other than the Christian is the religion of this country...In short, there is no charter or constitution that is either infidel, agnostic or non-Christian ... Christianity came to this country with the first colonists; has been powerfully identified with its rapid development, colonial and national, and today exists as a mighty factor in the life of the Republic. This is a Christian nation, and we can all rejoice."[1]

Powerful confirmation to those words can be found in the state constitutions of all 50 of these United States. Quotations from each of them are Appendix D of this book.

CHAMBERS OF
JUSTICE SANDRA DAY O'CONNOR

May 19, 1988

Ms. Annetta Conant
6380 E. Shiprock
Apache Junction, AZ 85219

Dear Neta,

You wrote me recently to inquire about any
holdings of this Court to the effect that this is a
Christian Nation. There are statements to such effect
in the following opinions:

Church of the Holy Trinity v. United
States,
143 U.S. 457 at 471 (1892);

Zorach v. Clauson,
343 U.S. 306 at 313 (1952);

McGowan v. Maryland,
366 U.S. 420 at 461 (1961).

I enclose a copy of the Church of the Holy
Trinity opinion as requested.

With best regards,

Sandra

34

One reason the modern American has such difficulty with the committed early Christians who settled this land is that they considered themselves God's Israel people. Scriptures such as Galatians 3:16 and 3:29 were written upon their hearts:

"Now to Abraham and his seed were the promises made. He saith not, And to seeds, as of many, but as of one, And to thy seed, which is Christ."

"And if you be Christ's, then are ye Abraham's seed, and heirs according to the promise."

Early American Christians could not foresee the flood of Dispensationalism which would ignore those scriptures in the 20th Century. They could not have known that an English lawyer, John Darby, would snatch the "rapture" doctrine from a Scottish lassie in 1830, and other Dispensational ideas from one Edward Irving.

Dave McPherson, author of *Rapture?* and *The Incredible Cover-up,* believes Dispensationalism originated with the Irvingites in Scotland, just as the "Pre-Tribulation Rapture" doctrine originated with Margaret Macdonald. The one "revelation" fed the other. Darby incorporated all these views into the Plymouth Brethren movement of the 19th Century, but McPherson contrasts British rejection of the key idea with American fascination of it as follows:

"Although the zealous Plymouth Brethren of Great Britain almost single-handedly planted British Pre-Tribism around the world during the last century (the sun never seems to set on their Eschatology Empire), *the same British evangelical group has largely abandoned Pre-Trib during the 20th Century.*"[2]

We predict that as America and the whole world plunge into chaotic times in this century's last decade, the vast majority of American believers will turn from both "Pre-Tribism" and "Christian Zionism" (the two key ideas of Dispensationalism). Not only are key predictions of Hal Lindsey's 31-million bestseller, *The Late Great Planet Earth,* now proven false, but a host of would-be prophets as well. One Edgar Whisenaut astounded many and sold 4 1/2 million copies of his books *88 Reasons* and *On Borrowed Time,* predicting that Christ would return during the Jewish New Year in September of 1988. A year later he set a second date. During press interviews when the 1989 date came, he admitted he was under medication for paranoid schizophrenia and offered alternate dates for the next few years!

God is raising up some powerful teaching to correct Dispensational errors. *Rapture! Prophecy or Heresy?* by Speed Wilson, has been recently released by Life Enrichment Publishers (P.O. Box 20050, Canton, OH 44701). Through word studies of the original Greek words in key New Testament passages, he shows how flimsy that whole eschatology is.

Missionary statesman John Bray, a non-Dispensational Baptist, also has some helpful booklets on both eschatology and Israel (P.O. Box 90129, Lakeland, FL 33804). Another non-Dispensational Baptist, the late Roy Newman, wrote the title chapter of *The Budding Fig Tree* in the NPL book we co-authored. He gave the scriptural case for the soon-destruction of Zionist Israel, a scenario which James McKeever of Omega Ministries has also predicted. God will raise up many voices for truth during this decade and beyond.

A vivid example of what happens to a believer steeped in truth when he encounters many Dispensationalists can be seen in *A Martyr Speaks,* journal of the late John Alan Coey. John was killed in Rhodesia in 1975, where he served as a fire-force medic during the war against the communist insurgency. An American who understood the treasonous facts of the Vietnam War disclosed in chapter 2 of his book, he could not in good conscience serve in Vietnam. But he wanted to defend Christian freedom; he was no coward. So he gave up his Marine Corps commission and flew to Rhodesia the day after he graduated from Ohio

State University in 1972.

A committed Christian, John sought out evangelical believers for fellowship. He probably knew many of the missionaries there on a first-name basis. He often went to their conferences. However, he realized that Dispensational imbalance was causing many to neglect key priorities. He wrote many articles during his three-year stay in Rhodesia. Some were published in mission magazines; some in military journals; some in patriot, free-press publications of both Rhodesia and South Africa. He also kept a journal of his observations, which was heavily censored after his death.

When Phyllis Coey, John's mother, sent me the journal for possible publication with NPL, she and her other son Ed had already filled in those censored time blocks with passages from letters sent home. There were also a few of John's articles in the stack of more than 500 pages of material. As soon as I got into it, I realized that John was a truly great thinker and writer who deserved to have an enormous impact on this and future generations. We asked Phyllis to come here for a week of work, and together she and I edited the material down to the 246-page book it is today. We chose as the first chapter John's article, "Christian Activism," originally published in a Baptist magazine in Rhodesia. Here are a few powerful paragraphs from it:

"Many Christians interpret these times as being the prelude to the Second Coming of Christ. There is convincing evidence that such events as the Zionist takeover of Palestine, the World Wars, the increase in knowledge and travel, the rise of Russia and communist conquests, the rise of the Ecumenical Church, occultism, and apostasy are the fulfillment of Biblical prophecy for the end times. It all seems to fit. Yet there is a strong argument that these things have happened before, such as during the collapse of the Roman Empire and during the Middle Ages; that

37

we are now witnessing the decline of Western civilization.

"At issue is a contest of faiths. We see the world in crisis because the impact of science and technology has displaced belief in the supernatural, faith in God. An alternative faith has arisen, the faith in man as the creative intelligence in the world, who by the force of his rational intelligence can re-direct his destiny and reorganize his life and world. By denying God, man becomes the most 'intelligent' of beings....

"It is said, the crisis of the Western World is the degree that it has separated itself from God, and shares the faith of the communists. The crisis of the Communist World is the degree it has failed to separate its people from God. The stronger faith will win."[3]

No one has ever said it more simply than that. Our crisis in America has come because we believers have allowed antichrist humanists to take over our land and dominate its agenda. We have lost perhaps 95% of our Constitutional freedom because of our apathy and preoccupation with our own personal lives and problems.

In such a time as this, what does Almighty God expect us to do?

After nearly fifteen years of seeking Him on this matter, and much fasting and prayer, I have come to one simple conclusion. Our God, who entered a covenant relationship with His people who established America, expects us to use the five percent of freedom we still have to gain back what we have lost!

Why? Because He cares far more than we do that His Great Commission be obeyed. The Lord Jesus Christ has an infinite love for every one of the 5-billion-plus people now living on this planet. It was His idea to provide America as a base of operation for His kingdom, not man's. Few Americans realize that roughly 57% of world missionary personnel and 85% of the funds for world evangelism come from America.

Are we saying that God's work here is purer or better than in other places? By no means! In fact, the cruel truth is that most in the American church have become God's "spoiled brats." No wonder our Father in heaven is about to take such children to the woodshed!

Yes, judgment is coming. It is unavoidable, even though fasting intercessors may have delayed it somewhat. Millions will doubtless lose their earthly lives. But one thing is certain. When Almighty God has brought His people out from the woodshed, there shall be a purified remnant.

Once when I spoke to a group in Johnstown, Pennsylvania, a woman there had a vision. She saw huge numbers of believers: men, women, and children in rags and without shoes, linked arm-in-arm as they marched in flanks, singing in praise and worship to God. I asked her to share what she saw with the men and women present. After she described her vision, she stopped a minute, then made this observation:

"Tonight I look out at this audience and see no one in rags or without shoes. In fact, I see people with lovely clothes, and much jewelry and make-up. However, I see *no one* with the *joy* on the faces of those believers in my vision!"

In the Old Testament, when people were unwilling to go where He wanted, He sent hornets to make them willing! That process has already begun in America. God is determined that His people will agree with Him.

"Can two walk together, except they be agreed?"[4]

Again, what does God expect of us?

"If my people, which are called by my name, shall humble themselves, and pray, and seek my face, and turn from their wicked ways; then shall I hear from heaven, and will forgive their sin, and will heal their land."[5]

There are two places where God's people must look if we are to meet His conditions for this crisis time: the book of *Joel,* and the record of how early Christians in America turned to Him.

Gone are the days when lone intercessors stand in the gap for the indifferent many! No, the *leaders and everyone in the surviving remnant* will humble themselves before the Almighty — or they will perish.

How *do* vast numbers of people humble themselves, pray, seek God's face, and turn from their wicked ways — all at the same time?

The corporate fast is the key. In Joel's prophecy, it turned doom into deliverance. In the writings of the early leaders, during the War of Independence and birth of our republic, several proclamations united the people in corporate fasting.

Here are excerpts from those of the *Continental Congress Journal:* June 12, 1775: "As the great Governor of the World, by his supreme and universal Providence...frequently influences the minds of man to serve the wise and gracious purpose of his providential government...This Congress recommends that Thursday, the 20th day of July next, be observed, by the inhabitants of all the English colonies on this continent, as a day of public humiliation, fasting, and prayer...And it is recommended to Christians, of all denominations, to assemble for public worship, and to abstain from servile labor and recreations on said day" (Vol. II, p. 87).

March 16, 1776: "In times of impending calamity and distress...it becomes the indispensable duty...with true penitence of heart, and the most reverent devotion, publickly to acknowledge the over-ruling providence of God; to confess and deplore our offenses against him...do earnestly recommend, that Friday, the 17th day of March next, be observed by the said colonies as a day of humiliation, fasting, and prayer..." (Vol. IV, pp. 208-209).

December 11, 1776: "...it becomes all public bodies, as well as private persons, to reverence the Providence of God, and look up to him as the supreme disposer of all events, and the arbitrator of the fate of nations. Resolved...to appoint a day of solemn fasting and humiliation; to implore of Almighty God the forgiveness of the many sins prevailing among all ranks..." (Vol. VI, p. 1022).

Corporate fasts were also called for in these journals on April 22, 1778; the first Thursday in May, 1779; April 26, 1780; April 3, 1781; the last Thursday in April 1782.

But these were not all. Many will cry out to God in their day of need. The truly Godly heritage that we have in America is nowhere more evident than the days set apart for *public thanksgiving and praise.* Here are some examples from the Journals of the Continental Congress:

November 1, 1777: "...it is the indispensable duty of all men to adore the superintending providence of Almighty God; to acknowledge with gratitude their obligation to him for benefits received, and to implore such further blessings as they stand in need of;...to set apart Thursday, the 18th day of December next, for solemn thanksgiving and praise..." (Vol. IX, pp. 854-55).

Similar days of thanksgiving and praise were called for December 30, 1778; December 9, 1779; December 7, 1781; November 28, 1782; the second Thursday in December 1783. In addition, Congress went to church en masse to thank God for the victory, at the end of the war!

October 24, 1781: "Resolved. That Congress will, at 2 o'clock today, go in procession to the Dutch Lutheran church, and return thanks to Almighty God, for crowning the allied arms of the United States and France, with success, by the surrender of the whole British army under the command of the Earl of Cornwallis" (Vol. XXI, p. 1071).

Under the current dominion of the secular humanist establishment in government and media, can we hear the outcry that would erupt with such a move, today? Imagine ACLU attorneys and NCC (National Council of Churches) pastors on national television to deplore this attack on "the separation of church and state"! Picture TV anchormen calling in Jews and Muslims, witches and atheists, to decry the insult to them inherent in such mass thanksgiving in a (horrors!) *Christian church*.

Samuel Adams wrote prophetic words about this sorry state of affairs in *Virtue and Knowledge*. "I have long been convinced that our Enemies have made it an Object, to eradicate from the Minds of the People in general a Sense of true Religion and Virtue, in hopes thereby the more easily to carry their Point of enslaving them" (April 30, 1776).

"If Heaven punishes Communities for their Vices, how sore must be the Punishment of that Community who thinks the Rights of human nature not worth struggling for and patiently submit to tyranny" (December 19, 1776). "...the more dearly we purchase our Liberties, the more we shall prize them and the longer we shall preserve them" (April 1, 1777).

"Our intelligence from England is very flattering to our Cause. They say we are fighting for the Liberty and Happiness of Mankind. We are at least contending for the Liberty and Happiness of our own Country and Posterity. It is a glorious Contest. We shall succeed if we are virtuous. I am infinitely more apprehensive of the Contagion of Vice than the Power of all other Enemies. It is the Disgrace of human nature that in most Countries the People are so debauched, as to be utterly unable to defend or enjoy their Liberty" (August 7, 1777).

"Our independence, I think, is secured. Whether America shall long preserve her Freedom or not, will depend upon her virtue" (December 21, 1778).

But perhaps the most arresting statement Adams made on the Constitutional crisis in which we find ourselves today was this fragmentary sentence of January 16, 1777: "Virtue, which is the Soul of republican government."

If the virtue is gone, can the republic survive?

Repentance, and a wholehearted return to the God of our forefathers is the only hope for our lives, our families, and our republic.

That process has begun.

Christian parents, in revulsion at the humanism and behavior modification being taught in our government schools, are providing alternate education. Home schooling is now in all 50 states, involving at least 5 million.

Then there is the Christian school movement. Roughly a decade ago I had the privilege of being a workshop leader during a national convention of ACSI (Association of Christian Schools International) held in Lancaster, Pennsylvania. There I heard the ACSI Executive Director Dr. Paul Kienel say, "If the present rate of Christian school beginnings continues, there will be no public schools by the year 2,000!"

Late in 1989 I taught on "America's Coming Crisis" at a church in Cincinnati, Ohio. A pastor present asked me after the meeting about God's plan for Israel in the coming scenario. Several others around him had similar questions. I asked if, by that, they were assuming the basic Dispensational tenet that the Jews are Israel. Since they were, I asked one of them to read Galatians 3:16 and 29, quoted earlier in this chapter.

It was evident that real insight came to the pastor. "I see," he said slowly. "If the whole premise of Dispensationalism is wrong, no deduction from it can possibly be right."

If enough believers wake up as he did in time, America may yet regain her freedom, and the whole specter of "Christian Zionism" will soon be distant history.

CHAPTER FOUR

CAN "CHRISTIAN ZIONISM" AND "JUDEO-CHRISTIANITY" SURVIVE GOD'S JUDGMENT?

By Dale Crowley, Jr.

According to C.I. Scofield [1843-1921], author of the Scofield Bible notes, Jesus came to this world to establish Himself as a Jewish king to rule over a Jewish kingdom, sitting on a Jewish throne in Jerusalem. But because His offer to the Jewish establishment of the day to reign over them was rejected, He changed His plan and decided to die on the cross instead, *postponing the Jewish Kingdom until a later date.*

Preposterous? Indeed.

According to the prophet Isaiah, Jesus would bear our griefs and carry our sorrows, and He would be wounded for our transgressions and bruised for our iniquities. Isaiah prophesied that a child would be born and a Son would be given, and that he would be called "Wonderful, Counselor, The mighty God, the everlasting Father, The Prince of Peace" (Isaiah chapters 53 and 9)...

The Roots of Christian Zionism

While we would simply prefer to dismiss Scofield's strange view that Jesus first pursued a Jewish political kingdom as outrageous and preposterous, unfortunately we are forced to challenge it because it is the root cause of pernicious Christian Zionism in the 20th Century.

Believe it or not, it is because Pat Robertson, Mike Evans, Jerry Falwell and Jimmy Swaggert believe that

Jesus Christ still has His eye on David's Jewish throne in order to rule over God's chosen people that they place reverential importance on the Jewish people, the state of Israel, and political/religious Zionism.

Never mind that Jesus is the eternal King whether First Century Jews agreed or not, or that He plainly taught that His Kingdom was "not of this world" (John 8:36), and that it was present among His hearers then and there (Luke 17:21), because, you see, what Jesus really wants now is to sit on that throne in Jerusalem that He aspired to nearly 20 centuries ago.

Never mind that the laws of Israel today discriminate against Christians, or that school children are taught not to use the plus sign for their arithmetic lessons because of its resemblance to the cross. You see, since Jesus will some day pick up where He left off, become King over God's chosen people in a Jewish kingdom, it is the televangelists' duty to expedite and facilitate the inception of that coming Jewish kingdom by supporting Jewish Israel now!

This is the stuff out of which modern Christian Zionism is made, and it can be found in black and white on the pages of the popular Scofield Reference Bible.

Today the Scofield doctrine that Jesus Christ "postponed" His reign over First Century Jews to a later date in the future is taught in 99 out of 100 Bible colleges and institutions in the United States and Canada. This explains why the graduates of these institutions, pastoring churches and speaking on radio and television Gospel programs, form the obedient front-line troops who blindly fight for Israel, preparing the way for that non-Christian nation to pay homage to Jesus Christ sitting on a throne in Jerusalem....[1]

Bible believers who do not subscribe to the Zionist-racist interpretation of Scripture were elated over reports in the International Edition of the *Jerusalem Post* (10/12/85) that Christians and Jews alike in Israel are sharply divided over the role of so-called Christian Zionism....

This "Zionist-racist interpretation of Scripture" can be defined in many ways. The essence of the heresy is that God has two groups of chosen people in the world: one, God's church, consisting of those who are spiritually linked to God, and the other, the physical descendants of Israel (Jacob), who have no such link to God. (To many Zionist/ racist Christians, God is more interested in the latter than the former.)

While many interpreters of Scripture see the sweeping movement in support of unbelieving Israel as one of the evidences of end-time deception, they also believe that sooner or later the heresy of Christian Zionism/racism must be exposed, and will, accordingly, be abandoned.

This is where the International Christian Embassy in Jerusalem comes in. This pro-Israel, Christian Zionist organization was, according to *Jerusalem Post,* "torn by dissent," and "practicing excommunication" of the dissenters. Others have "either resigned or been forced to leave."

The most immediate effect of these ruptures in the supposedly solid front of the Christian Zionists was the "boycotting" of the Feast of Tabernacles celebration by "well-known Christian evangelical figures."

The Christian Embassy was founded in Jerusalem in 1980 on the premise that the Lord will bless the modern state of Israel, despite the fact that it is militantly anti-Christian, and has even passed laws designed to halt missionary endeavor.

The disruption in the harmony among Christian Zionists seems to be the result of a disagreement on purpose. Two leaders in Jerusalem, Messrs. Jan Willem Van Der Hoeven and Johann Luckoff, want to stick to the work of "comforting Zion," while leaders in England, the U.S., Canada, and New Zealand want to do more than comfort Zion, and take the love of Christ a step further toward reconciliation between Jews and Arabs. The Jerusalem headquarters, however, openly supporting the Likud (Begin/Shamir/Sharon) Party, could hardly take a position of reconciliation and peace.

Evidence of these cracks in the wall of worldwide Christian Zionism were also seen at the 1985 Christian Zionist Congress held in Basel, Switzerland. Concerning that, Pinna Peli said the following in that *Jerusalem Post* article:

"Calling a Christian Zionist Congress...smacks of over-identification, verging on willful substitution, taken for granted by many Christians.

"The people of Israel can no longer afford to underestimate the relentless determination of the other monotheistic religions to take over its rightful inheritance, historical and geographical.

"The Embassy-sponsored *Voice of Hope* radio station... has been blatantly missionary in its broadcasts since its inception....

"While the state must guarantee the free expression and integrity of all faiths and systems of belief, Israel has no obligation to promote or even tolerate either Moslem imperialism or Christian triumphalism. Only in this spirit can Jerusalem be rebuilt, speedily and in our days."

That says it all for the political/religious philosophy of most of the leaders and citizens of Israel. The first part of Miss Peli's fearful last concept is mutually exclusive of the last part. A state cannot guarantee "the free exercise of religion" on the one hand, and refuse to tolerate the evangelistic efforts of any and all religions on the other....[2]

Israel Shahak, Professor of Chemistry at Hebrew University, a survivor of the Bergen-Belsen Concentration Camp, gave me the following information which I published in a paper and distributed through *The King's Business* radio program:

"Dishonoring Christian religious symbols is an old religious duty in Judaism. Spitting on the cross, and especially on the crucifix, and spitting when a Jew passes a church, were obligatory for hundreds of years (from around 200 A.D.) on pious Jews. In the past, when the danger of anti-Semitism was a real one, the pious Jews were commanded by their rabbis either to spit so that the reason for doing so would be unknown, or to spit into their bosoms, not actually on the cross or openly before the church.

"The increasing strength of the Jewish state caused those customs to become more open again, but there should be no mistake: The spitting on the cross for *converts from Christianity to Judaism* organized in Kibbutz Sa'ad and financed by the Israeli government is an act of traditional Jewish piety. It does not cease to be barbaric, horrifying and wicked because of this. On the contrary, it is worse because it is so traditional, and much more dangerous as well, just as the renewed anti-Semitism of the Nazis was dangerous because, in part, it played on the traditional anti-Semitic past.

"This barbarous attitude of contempt and hate to Christian symbols has grown in Israel, first slowly, and in the last years very rapidly....

"Other little known laws against Christianity are these:

"Churches cannot be built in any Jewish settlement, villages, towns, or cities new or old.

"There is a five-year prison sentence for anyone who preaches the Gospel, and accompanies the preaching with materials, books, medicine, food, clothing, scholarship or travel grants, etc.

"Well-known missionaries who are on Israel's black list are permitted to stay in Israel only six weeks, or they may be denied entrance and ordered to leave at the airport."

Haviv Schieber gave me this additional information on Israeli persecution of Christians, which I published in the same sheet:

"In 1954 the Chief Rabbi of Tel Aviv ordered the destruction of the Southern Baptist Church, which had been built with all necessary building permits.

"In Tel Aviv today Christian missions are blackmailed, attacked, and burned.

"On Friday, October 2, 1982, the Jerusalem Baptist Church was burned to the ground. *The Washington Post* gave the news two inches of space on page 26 of its October 9 issue."

So much for Zionist "religious liberty" and persecution of Christians. Now let us apply God's searchlight to the euphemistic term, "Judeo-Christian."

"Judeo-Christian" is a term invented by Christians; Judaists would never do such a thing. It can be explained in one of two ways, or both: (1) A misguided notion that says that the Old Testament belongs to Judaism, or (2) A sop to throw to the Judaists to seek their goodwill.

Neither is acceptable....

There was a time when I really did not understand the uniquely Christian heritage of America, either. I sincerely and confidently used the self-contradictory term that I had heard, "Judeo-Christian."

Perhaps a listing of some of the most fundamental keys to the understanding of the Bible would serve to unlock this barrier, and enable us never again to use the phrase, "America's Judeo-Christian heritage."

1. The Old Testament pointed to the events of the New Testament.

2. The central character of the Old Testament is the promised Messiah.

3. Saving faith in the Old Testament was the same as saving faith in the New Testament: that is, the same kind of faith as father Abraham had.

4. Saving faith in the Old Testament predated the appearance of the Israelites, Moses, the Laws, and the religion of the Jews.

5. God's saving grace in the Old Testament extended to the same people as His saving grace in the New Tes-

tament: that is, to the believing "remnant" of any racial background.

6. The descendants of Abraham, Isaac, and Jacob of Old Testament times who understood Old Testament Scriptures readily believed in Jesus Christ. These understanding, believing Jews included Zacharias and Elizabeth, Joseph and Mary, the shepherds, Simeon and Anna, John the Baptist, and many others.

7. The descendants of Abraham, Isaac, and Jacob of Old Testament times who *did not* understand the Old Testament Scriptures disbelieved and opposed our Lord Jesus Christ, John the Baptist, and the Apostles.

8. Our Lord's major antagonists during His ministry on earth were those who did not believe the Old Testament Scriptures, but had substituted their own traditions instead. (The oral traditions of the elders were later written down in the *Talmud* from the 2nd to the 7th century A.D. — the basis of modern Judaism.)

9. Among the Apostle Paul's major antagonists were those who did not see the true spiritual implications of the Old Testament Scriptures upon the events of the first century. Inspired by the Holy Spirit, he based his writings entirely upon the Old Testament....

A fundamental tenet of the Christian faith is that the Old and New Testaments are a harmonious unit, setting forth the holiness, justice, love, and saving grace of Jehovah God. God's love and saving grace were extended to the Gentile nations through the Hebrew Old Testament scriptures, while the writers and readers of the Greek New Testament Scriptures in the early years were mainly Hebrew Christians. During the transition (the events reported in Matthew, Mark, Luke, John and the Acts), the Hebrew Old Testament Scriptures were the *only* Scriptures available and in use. During those days *only* those descendants of Jacob who correctly understood the Hebrew Old Testament believed in Jesus and built His church.

There are not two sets of Scriptures (for two groups of people) upon which America was established. America's heritage is Christian, the outcome of the Hebrew Scriptures, Genesis 1:1 through Revelation 22:21...

Judaism is not the religion of the Old Testament. It is a religion created by the priests and scribes who discarded the *Torah* (Old Testament law), killed God's prophets, and instituted their own religious dogmas and ceremonies in the *Talmud.*

The *Talmud* is pure rebellion against Jehovah God. It shows how a man can violate a 3-year-old girl and not be punished; how a priest can hire the services of a prostitute in the temple and not be punished; how a Jew can murder a Gentile and not be punished; how a man can break all his agreements and vows and not be punished *(Kol Nidre).* It will also tell you about the "private life" of Jehovah!

Dr. Jacob Gartenhaus, beloved Christian evangelist and scholar, uses these words in his description of the *Talmud:* "Ridiculous tales," "ludicrous speculation," "obscene jokes," "obnoxious desires," "strange words," "absurdities," "pure nonsense," and "one of the world's strangest and most confused books, or set of books." (Write King's Business Ministries, P.O. Box One, Washington, DC 20044 for a copy of Dr. Gartenhaus' article and/or my booklet, *Christian! Not Judeo-Christian.)*

Does Talmudic Judaism play any role in our 20th Century "Judeo-Christian ethic"?

The answer to that question is, unfortunately and ironically, "Yes." And our preachers and politicians who mouth those oh-so-pleasing words don't realize the extent to which they are admitting and sharing in the betrayal of America.

A long line of Talmudic Jewish rabbis, financiers, philosophers, psychologists, sociologists, educators, lawyers, judges, economists, and other intellectuals, media owners and personalities, publishers and writers, have very nearly turned this nation from its Old and New Testament heritage. Indeed, the roots of situational ethics, moral relativism, spiritual rebellion, and humanism that are destroying America today come from the pages of the *Talmud*.[3]

Recently a story appeared in the *Washington Jewish Week* (10/12/89) headlined "Jews on TV. More and more, Jews are in front of the camera."

This is an astonishing development. The Jews are doing the very same thing that they have been jumping on us for years for doing.

Ted Pike has been castigated for daring to tell the truth about the Jewish domination of Hollywood and the media in his book, *Israel: Our Duty, Our Dilemma,* and his video, *The Other Israel.* [He is based at the National Prayer Network, P.O. Box 203, Oregon City, OR 97045.] Recently Norman Lear has called Pike "anti-Semitic."

Cardinal Glemp of Poland was recently charged with anti-Semitism merely because he stated what we all know to be true — that in any dispute the Jews have the advantage because they control world mass communications.[4]

This control has produced an open sewer in the so-called entertainment world of New York and Hollywood. Recently the preoccupation with sex and violence has moved ever deeper into evil with open blasphemy. Of the film, *The Last Temptation of Christ,* the radical rabbi, Meir Kahane, has this surprisingly accurate analysis:

"Lew Wasserman is a Jew. He is head of a huge Hollywood entertainment conglomerate which includes Universal Studios, that produced *Last Temptation*....For Hollywood and Wasserman, nothing is sacred, nothing is beyond the pale, nothing is forbidden. There is no such thing as good taste or any taste for that matter; there is no concern for respect of feelings and emotions and faith. People such as Wasserman, who daily genuflect before the altar of Mammon (money), do not have any concept of ideals and deep-felt beliefs....

"Little does the tiny Lew Wasserman realize the extent of the flood of hatred he has unleashed...Jerry Falwell, leader of the evangelicals, predicted a wave of anti-Semitism by Christians who would blame Jews and 'Jewish leaders.' ...The Italian director Franco Zeffireli withdrew his own film from the Venice Festival in protest against the scheduled screening there of *Temptation*. He attacked the 'Jewish cultural scum of Los Angeles' that he said were 'always spoiling for a chance to attack the Christian world'...

"The lessons of this ugly, sordid story are basic. Let us learn them:

"1. The assimilated Jew, the one who leaves his people and attempts to dissolve into the Gentile society in which he exists, is invariably the one who will bring down on the people from whom he fled, all the latent Jew-hatred of the majority — a majority that sees in the fleeing, assimilated Jew, nothing except a Jew. The Jew can, ultimately, never flee his Jewishness and Judaism. At best, he will be destroyed. At worst, he brings down on all Jews the horrors and punishment for his actions.

"2. America is not a melting pot. It is not a haven for the Jew. America is a land of Christians who, no matter how little they may practice their faith at any given moment, are, in the end, Christians who bitterly resent non-Christians who blaspheme and offend their faith...

"Any effort by the Jew to de-Christianize America will not only not succeed, but it will so enrage Christians as to bring about an explosion of terrible Jew-hatred...

"That is why efforts on the part of the American Jewish Establishment groups to prevent official Christmas presentations or creches or figurines or trees on public property may win short-range victories but at the expense of long-range disaster. That is why when one reads that, in England, Jews are infuriated by the fact that the Post Office has marked almost all letters with the words "Jesus

Is Alive,'' one shakes his head in sad dismay. All the angry protests by the British Jews miss the point that England is a Christian country and if Christians in Israel would object to Jewish slogans and Judaization of the country, normal Jews would quite properly rise up in indignation.

"If a Christian wishes to live in Israel, he must accept that he is living in a Jewish country. The same holds true for the Jew. If he willingly chooses to live in a Christian land, let him know it and not attempt to change it. On the one hand, he cannot. On the other, he will bring down, on himself and his people, tragedy."[5]

Quite a prophetic word from this Orthodox Jewish rabbi, member of the Israeli Knesset, and founder of the major Zionist terrorist organization in the U.S., the Jewish Defense League.

Our Life With Haviv Schieber

One of the most fateful and momentous events in my life was that morning in 1982 when God led me to accept an invitation from Haviv Schieber to have coffee with him at the S&W cafeteria in Falls Church, Virginia.

He had heard about me, and decided to try to recruit me to be a member of his little loosely knit band of anti-Zionist warriors. He never wearied in this activity, and in the last years of his life I called him, "General."

At first I was suspicious of him. But we grew to be trusting and loyal friends. I learned the meaning of *chutzpah* from Haviv.

I was often annoyed with his impetuousness, high-handedness, presumption, and just plain rudeness. But I never once doubted that God had given me the great privilege and responsibility of helping and ministering to this marvelous man, the likes of which I had never met in all my life.

It was my privilege and honor to do the following at

the behest of the "General": Edit his Yiddish-sounding English, and prepare camera-ready copy for the printer; be his chauffeur, driving him between his home in Fairfax, my home in Annandale, Metro subway stops everywhere, his office in Washington, and the offices of his high-level Arab and Palestinian friends all over town; help him distribute ("DIS-tri-bute") his materials and carry his signs and placards at strategic points.

I learned so much from Haviv on every topic imaginable relative to Israelites and the Jews — the Bible, history, Communism, Israel, Zionism, etc. He never tired of teaching this "stupid Gentile" (as he sometimes called me) about his "Jewish brethren."

"Oh Dale," he would sometimes exclaim with emotion, "My people love to hate." Or, "Zionism is Jewish Naziism."

When I would commend him on his frequent flashes of brilliance and logic, he would say, "It's nothing. Two plus 2 equals 4. My Jewish brethren try to make 2 plus 2 equal 5."

He told me of his boyhood in Poland, and how his family fled the Bolsheviks, of how he believed Hitler and then worked to get Jews out of Germany (while most Jews opted to stay). He told me of his early years in Israel with Begin, Shamir, and Zionism. He told me of his conversion to Jesus Christ in 1956 after the rabbis had destroyed a building he had constructed for the local Baptist church. He told me of his struggle with the INS, the Justice Department, and the hated OSI of the FBI, and with other Zionists and fellow Jews in high levels in the U.S. government.

In August 1985 Haviv collapsed in his home with a massive invasion of cancer in his intestines. He nearly died on the operating table. His recovery was slow, but within a few weeks he was back out on the streets.

Mary and I took him in at our missionary hospitality home in Arlington, "Temporarily." But Haviv told someone else that that's where he'd live the rest of his life. We weren't happy with that prospect, but again, we were convinced that this was one of God's special people, and that our mission was to serve him during the last years of his life.

On several occasions Mary said to him, "Haviv, with you here in our house, I'm afraid we're going to be bombed."

He had two standard responses: One, that with him in our house it could not be more safe, because his "Jewish brethren" were determined to ignore him. Or two, "Oh, would to God they would bomb me, and stop ignoring me."

Haviv was thrilled when I started my *Focus On Israel* radio program in the summer of 1986. He appeared with me often on that program, and some of his messages were printed in *Christian News*. But by the summer of '87 Haviv's vigorous voice was gone, and he told me he didn't want his enemies to hear him speak with a weak voice.

Haviv predicted the *Intifada* (i.e., Palestinian uprising), but he died the very month it began. To my surprise, he had no interest in seeing it on television. He was too weak.

On December 31, 1987, I left for the office and said "Goodbye" to Haviv. Later that morning he told his pastor, Stephen King of the Cherrydale Baptist Church in Arlington, "Today I will be with Jesus." In the afternoon an Arlington County volunteer nurse watched him sink into a coma. That's how I found Haviv when I returned home in the evening. I wanted to pray and read the Bible with him one more time, but it was too late. It was hard for me to accept that this brave soldier whom I never knew to give up or quit, was going to leave us. I still believed that he would regain consciousness.

But around 6:00 p.m. Haviv gasped his last breath, closed his eyes slowly, and was still. I said, "Haviv, I'll see you again on the other side."

Suddenly Haviv opened his eyes, wide, very wide. They were bigger and clearer, and more focused than I had ever seen them before. (During the coma his eyes were blurred and wandering.) I thought he was coming back to life.

But he remained motionless, gazing heavenward for about a minute, seemingly awestruck. I realized that Haviv was being received into the glorious presence of our Lord Jesus Christ.

Then his eyes closed slowly again for the last time and, though dead, the corners of his mouth turned up into a smile. He knew that he had won his last great battle.

Truly, as in life, his departure was spectacular.

But Haviv wasn't through with the world, or his "Jewish brethren." For two more weeks we had to struggle with a Rockville, Maryland rabbi and the Arlington Hospital, in a Virginia court, for the right to bury him in accordance with his instructions — in a Christian funeral, and with his Christian friends. (Write me for this amazing episode, "To Steal an anti-Zionist Jew," available in mid-1990: P.O. Box 1, Washington, DC 20044.)

CHAPTER FIVE

THE TESTIMONY OF THE LATE HAVIV SCHIEBER

with Len Martin

I was born and raised in the commercial city of Lwow, Poland, by middle class Jewish parents. My family, while not truly orthodox, was nevertheless quite religious. I was educated in private Hebrew grade and high schools, and received biblical tutoring from a rabbi....

In 1927, at the age of fourteen, I joined a Jewish youth movement which changed my life radically, and irrevocably. It was called *Betar*....

Betar was the youth "arm" of the Revisionist New Zionist Organization. We were fanatic in our efforts to secure a Jewish state in Palestine. Even our uniforms were symbolic: the dark brown of the soil of Palestine. The words to my favorite song were:

The two banks of Jordan must be ours,
The Arabs can shoot and blood can flow,
But Transjordan, Transjordan is ours!

Transjordan was the land now known as Jordan.

I was tremendously dedicated to the Zionist cause. During my high school years in Poland, I had but one goal: to graduate and then immigrate to Palestine.

One incident from my years with the Polish *Betar* stands out in my memory with great clarity. Soon after I joined the group, I participated in a mass rally with several hundred other Jews. The occasion was the anniversary of the signing of the Balfour Declaration, in which the British promised a homeland in Palestine to the Jews. We all marched to the British Consulate in Lwow to cheer and voice our thanks to England for the favor they had done us Jews.

It was not until years later that I learned that the "favor" the English had done for the Jews was just the British half of a bargain. In return for the support of Chaim Weizmann and the Zionist leadership in getting the United States to enter World War I on the British side, the British had agreed to throw their influence behind the establishment of the Jewish homeland in Palestine. With the Balfour Declaration, the British were just honoring their part of the bargain. But during the demonstration, I was blissfully unaware of all this. I was just happy that eventually we Jews would have a land of our own...

Communist Cells In Jewish Schools

I must emphasize that at this time *the only communist cells in Poland were found in Jewish schools.* It is no wonder that the Polish people call the Polish Communist Party *Zydo Komuna* or "Jewish Communism."

Through my involvement in high school activities, I discovered that nearly all of the Polish Communists *were Jews.* This puzzled me for some years until I came to realize that *Communist activity* in Europe *was carried on* primarily *by Jews.* Karl Marx, founder and major philosopher of Utopian Communism, was a Jew. After the Russian Revolution, Trotsky, Kaminev, Zinowiev, Radik and Kaganovich (all Jews) held or rose to some of the most powerful positions in the new Soviet regime. The first Soviet Politburo was composed of three Jews and two Gentiles; and two Jews and one Gentile composed the second. Also, Jews held many important positions in the Soviet bureaucracy...

The appeal of Communism to certain portions of world Jewry is two-fold:

First, Marxist Communism promises to destroy religion, "the opiate of the masses." During the 19th and early part of the 20th centuries, some Christian Gentiles, especially in Eastern Europe, used the Christmas and Easter holidays for anti-Jewish activities. Some used words, others violence in attacking Jews as Christ killers or unbelievers. The ensuing mob scenes, as usual, made good cover to vendettas. These Jews reasoned that if Communism destroyed all religion, Christ would be discredited and Jews would have no more Christian persecutors.

Born Internationalists

Secondly, Jews are born internationalists. In Eastern Europe especially, Jews felt no nationalistic loyalties: they were Jews first, and citizens second. Without a homeland, their first loyalty was to the race. Communism promised to create a one-world government with all allegiance owed solely to the world state. As the Jews saw it, Communism would eliminate nations — and thus eliminate national hatreds, national insecurity and the pressure of national loyalty....

Zionism, as defined by the 1975 edition of the *New Webster's Dictionary,* is "a modern plan or movement to colonize Hebrews [sic] in Palestine, the land of Zion; a movement to secure for such Jews as cannot or will not be assimilated in the country of their adoption a national home in Palestine, part of which now forms the State of Israel."

The true history of spiritual Zionism begins with the Second Diaspora or dispersal of the Jews after the destruction of the Second Temple, an event recorded in the Bible.

For 2000 years, Orthodox Jews and religious Spiritual Zionists have maintained that the Jewish race has no business in the ex-Promised Land, the Holy Land, until the coming of their Messiah. During these 20 centuries, many pious Jews have gone to Palestine to pray for their brothers and for the appearance of their Messiah....

Political Zionism was started by Theodor Herzl, a totally assimilated Austrian Jewish journalist. While covering the infamous Dreyfus case in France, he became horrified at the tremendous anti-Jewish feeling the trial created in a supposedly civilized country. In 1895 he wrote *Der Judanstaat (The State of the Jews)* in which he pictured in Palestine a safe haven for Jews. In 1897, he called the first World Jewish Congress in Basel, Switzerland. It was at this Congress that the World Zionist Organization was born....

When Herzl died in 1904, Russian and Polish Jews took over the World Zionist Organization. During World War I a Polish Jew, Chaim Weizmann, became its leader.

After the Balfour Declaration in 1917, political Zionism began to gain strength among world Jewry. As they stepped up their promotion of immigration to the Holy Land, *Russian Marxist Jews* took over political leadership in Palestine and began to dominate all Zionist institutions.

A major split occurred in the World Zionist Organization in 1933. Vladamir Jabotinsky, the man who had formed the Zionist youth organization, *Betar,* rebelled against the Marxist policies of the World Zionist Organization. His anti-Communist Revisionist Zionist faction formed the New Zionist Organization, but this anti-Communist movement collapsed. During World War Two, its members started the present-day right-wing Likud Party in Israel.

Today's World Zionist Organization contains three main factions:

A. *The Marxist Zionists* This is the dominant force, having the most members and most of the political power.

B. *The General Zionists* Not allied with any political

ideology. This group contains the Religious Zionists.

C. *The Likud* The right wing anti-Communist faction is the remnant of Jabotinsky's Revisionist movement. It has the least power and fewest members.

All these factions, in general, follow the Marxist/Socialist economic system in Israel, making it a beggar state. This has led to economic and moral bankruptcy....

My Life In Palestine Begins

During the years 1928-36, there was great tension in Palestine. The Marxist-Zionists and we anti-Communist Zionists were having daily battles in the streets. Unfortunately for us, the Marxist faction had the full support of the World Zionist Organization and the Jewish agency. Also, the Marxist-Zionists had the support of the labor organization (the *Histadrut),* and the commune settlements (the *Kibbutzim)* which were large and had substantial financial backing.

Because our organization was highly critical of British politics in Palestine, the British authorities tended to ignore the terrorism directed against us by Marxist-Zionists led by Ben Gurion and Golda Meir.

In 1934, the Marxist-Zionists in Palestine were busy with a massive campaign to depose the anti-Nazi Austrian Chancellor, Dolfus. Our group opposed their collection of money in Palestine because it would be sent to the *Schutzbund,* the Austrian Socialist Party which, like most National Socialist parties, was dominated by Marxist Jews. Our opposition was also based on the fact that we recognized Hitler as a terrible threat to the Jews. Dolfus was anti-Hitler....

Marxist-Zionists Play Ball With Hitler

It was the Marxist-Zionist organization in Palestine that was directly responsible for the many Jews who were killed or sent to the concentration camps in Europe during World War II. I do not make this statement lightly. It is one of the terrible realities of history that the Marxist-Zionists have succeeded in keeping suppressed.

When Hitler came to power in 1933 the Marxist-Zionists' first action was to sign the "Transfer Pact" with him. They signed this agreement with full knowledge of what Hitler promised to do to European Jews. The terms of the pact were that any Jews wishing to emigrate from Germany would be free to do so, providing that:

1. They would only go to Palestine;

2. They took nothing but personal belongings with them;

3. The German government would appraise the value of all the emigrating Jews' remaining property.

4. Payment of the evaluation be made to the emigrating Jews in the form of German Government Bonds: 30% in so-called "Blue" bonds and 70% in "White" bonds. The "Blue" bonds were exchangeable or redeemable in metals, and the "White" bonds were redeemable in ceramics and fabrics. Germany had a surplus of these products and was trying to export them to help finance its war machine.

In addition to negotiating the pact, the World Zionist Organization and the Jewish Agency, both Marxist dominated, handled the financial aspects of all emigration of Jews to Palestine.

Faced with these conditions, few German Jews would agree to go to Palestine. Most of these Jews preferred to stay, blindly believing that Hitler could eventually be bought. The Marxist-Zionists promoted this blind trust that Hitler could be bought, and spread this belief to Jews in other threatened European countries.

In opposition to Hitler's harsh economic treatment of German Jews, we anti-Marxist Zionists in Palestine proclaimed a boycott of German goods. Since we were such a small minority, our efforts and warnings were of little avail....

Israel Under The Marxist-Zionists

May 1, 1949 [a year after Israel was recognized as a state by the UN - Ed.] was a red letter day for Israel. David Ben Gurion and Golda Meir issued a proclamation that in one year, May 1, 1950, Israel was to become a full-fledged Socialist state with its capital to be Jerusalem. Ben Gurion then sent Golda Meir and Mr. Namir to Moscow as Israel's first ambassadors. The choice was apt. No one in the entire government was a more fanatical Marxist than Golda Meir; and Mr. Namir was General Secretary of the Marxist labor union, the *Histadrut,* which controlled Israel's economic and labor policies. In Moscow, in May 1949, this satanic pair made a secret agreement with Stalin and his right-hand man, Kaganovich. Israel's part in this agreement was:

1. Israel would not allow any Western country, especially the U.S., to build military bases in Israeli territory;

2. Israel would allow an official Communist Party to function freely;

3. Israel would *not* make agreements to solve the Palestinian refugee problems;

4. Israel would influence World Jewry, especially in the U.S., to have Western powers adopt a policy favoring Israel over Arabs; and,

5. Israel was to continue Marxist economic policies and prevent free enterprise tendencies.

To understand the reasoning for this madness, the treacherous mentalities of the parties involved must be understood. The Soviets and Marxist Jews wished to prevent peace between the Arab countries and Israel until all the Arab countries adopted Socialism under Soviet leadership....

Communist Jews And Their Future

Here I wish to add a comment about current events. In the last several years, there has been increasing hue and cry about freeing Soviet Jewry...This mass exodus could be used to infiltrate legions of totally dedicated Soviet agents and agitators all over the world....

In time, I grew tired of these scarcely veiled threats and constant harassment and decided to fight. I organized the Anti-Communist League of Israel and the Democratic Party of Israel....

In spite of all this activity and government interference, our organizations, the Anti-Communist League and the Democratic Party had finished the big housing project in Jaffa. Everything but the last room was completed and occupied.

The group in charge of hampering our construction was called the militia of Apotropus. This was the Israeli agency in charge of abandoned property. The day before Yom Kippur, the Day of Atonement, when I thought they would be busy elsewhere, we tried to finish the last room.

One of my men noticed a bearded man observing us and then making a telephone call. Shortly, a group of Apotropus thugs appeared and started destroying the work we had done that day. Extremely angered, I grabbed a concrete block and was about to hit one of the militia men, when a strange thing happened.

I heard a voice say: "Put down the stone and come to me." Immediately, I thought I had heard the voice of Jesus. Call it hallucination, imagination or whatever, but to me it was very real. Whatever it was, it had an instant calming effect on me. I sat down and watched quietly, without anger and resentment, as the militia destroyed our work.

The day after Yom Kippur, I went to the headquarters of the Militia and said to the commander: "Thank you for the demolition of our work. In doing so you have brought me to Jesus Christ..."

The Marxist group that controls Israel today is the same radical Jewish element that couldn't fit in with the Jewish Trotskyites in Moscow after the Bolshevik Revolution. Their solution: Migration to Israel. While this clique followed Marxist ideology, they were independent from Moscow. To the outside world, they identified their Communist/Socialist practices as not Communism but Socialist Zionism...

My experience with the voice of Jesus left me with a great thirst for knowledge. For the first time, I read the New Testament of the Bible. The parallels between the time of Jesus and the modern day in Israel were amazing...

Democracy In Israel — The Big Lie

In 1953, in an effort to mount a drive to gain political strength, the Democratic Party of Israel entered a slate of candidates for the Knesset (Israel's Parliament) called "Ex-Servicemen and Newcomers." Since in Israel, all paper supplies must come from the government, each party was allowed only a limited amount of election publicity.

After we had all our posters and campaign material printed, our top candidate was falsely accused and arrested for selling some of our paper. This stopped our campaign before it even got started.

This experience finally convinced our Anti-Communist League that there was no chance of changing the system in Israel from within. Every attempt to replace the Marxist-Zionist government in Israel with a free democratic one would be frustrated. There was no political party existing in Israel that had a positive alternative plan to bring about political and economic change. *All popular Israeli parties were fingers of the same hand. This is as true today as it was then...*

The plan that the Anti-Communist League of Israel proposed to all groups with whom we were in contact was this:

First, create a world-embracing group called the Anti-Communist International. It would have no government affiliations and members would act as private citizens.

Second, launch a massive propaganda campaign aimed behind the Iron Curtain. The campaign would be two-fold. Primarily, it would tell the citizens of the "captive nations" not to depend on Western help in gaining their freedom. It would also suggest ways in which they could, clandestinely or otherwise, encourage the breakdown of the fragile Communist social and economic systems. Then, by showing the material advantages of free enterprise and democracy, we would hope to motivate people in the Communist bloc to keep constant pressure on the totalitarian regimes.

As more and more people clamored for return of business from state control to private hands and demand more food and luxury items, we believed that Communism would begin to collapse without the need for a bloody, useless revolution....

[A vast section of Schieber's book, *Holy Land Betrayed,* deals with his subsequent experiences and decision to emigrate to the United States. We pick up the story in 1966, when he was in New York. — Ed.]

Increased Activities

Once back in New York, I stepped up my anti-Communist activities. During Captive Nations Week in 1966, Anti-Communist International organized the biggest demonstration against the Soviet Union that New York had ever witnessed. All the media was present to cover the event; yet, not a word was printed or heard, or a picture seen of our protest. Of course, this is understandable — the news media is controlled by the Zionists.

This is something that every anti-Communist group struggles with, even today. The Communists rate front-page headlines with their day-to-day affairs, but a rally with participation of thousands of patriots is invariably ignored by the heavily Zionist-influenced American news media...

The Solution — A Holy Land State

I believe God's plan is this: Israel should disarm, throw open her borders, and adopt a free enterprise system. This is the only way that massive destruction, perhaps involving global nuclear war, can be averted.

If Israel were to open her borders and disarm, backed by international guarantees of security, the Arabs would not take advantage of the state of disarmament. The Arabs do not wish to fight and die for a "cause" when there is no longer a threat to them. The Palestinians would return and, under a free enterprise system with international assistance, be given back what is rightfully theirs.

Under a free economic system, the port cities of the Holy Land would once again become centers of trade and would contain pipelines for Arab oil, as they once were. Foreign capital and investment would flow again if the government did not demand 51% of an investment enterprise. Finally, and most importantly, Jews would rule jointly with Christians and Moslem Arabs in the Holy Land. There would be complete religious, political and social freedom once again. Jabotinsky's famous prophecy in his song would be fulfilled in a Holy Land state.

"In our country, a son of Nazareth
a son of Araby and my son
will live in happiness and prosperity."

This is the essence of my new dream. I am as dedicated to it as I had been to my childhood dream of a Jewish state.

CHAPTER SIX

ANTI-SEMITISM

By Des Griffin

ANTI-SEMITISM! Like cold, clammy hands closing around their throats, that charge strikes terror into the hearts of most Americans.

ANTI-SEMITISM! For the vast majority, it is a label to be avoided at all costs. It must be warded off with greater fervor than AIDS, cancer or some other deadly disease. Like one suffering from leprosy in ancient times, anyone thought to be suffering from this dread disease is considered a social outcast, an individual to be shunned by one and all.

When one has AIDS one is looked upon with mercy and compassion by our modern, highly sophisticated and "understanding" society. If, on the other hand, one is labeled as being "anti-Semitic," one is rejected, spurned and socially cast into outer darkness. Anti-Semitism is considered a more deadly disease than AIDS....

Anti-Semitism

Since late in the last century shrieking cries of "anti-Semitism" and "anti-Jew" have echoed and reverberated around the world. Early in this century, several heavily financed organizations, such as the Anti-Defamation League of B'nai B'rith (ADL) and the American Civil Liberties Union (ACLU), were established for the specific purpose of countering "anti-Semitism." In recent decades,

71

movie and television producers have also made a lot of financial hay from the subject. They have produced a continuous stream of movies and TV specials that capitalize on the alleged wrongs inflicted upon Jews in recent decades. Book publishers have also jumped on the bandwagon, with great financial success. In addition, the Zionist state of Israel is kept afloat financially by welfare payments (approximately $4,000,000,000 annually from the United States alone!) extorted under the shield of this propaganda blitz. There is big money in them thar ''anti-Semitic'' hills!

Anyone who has had the gall to raise the Jewish issue and pose serious questions on the subject, has been condemned as unconscionably wicked and obviously suffering from mental aberrations. They are automatically dubbed as being ''anti-Semitic,'' ''rabidly anti-Jewish'' and ''conscious practitioners of deceit and malice.''

As eleven-term Congressman Paul Findley of Illinois proves in his book, *They Dare To Speak Out,* many reputations have been sullied, if not altogether destroyed, by such smear tactics. Additional thousands maintain a stoic silence for fear of the Jews. They fear that their reputations will be ruined if they utter as much as a squeak on the subject.

Facts Are Facts

The anti ''anti-Semitism'' propaganda blitz has had a major impact on the thinking of the American public in recent decades. In fear of being stigmatized as bigots and rabid anti-Semites, many Americans have avoided any serious consideration of the Jewish issue. Most choose to ignore the subject.

Benjamin Freedman, a Jew who was on a first name basis with most of the top Zionists in the 1930s and 40s, puts his finger firmly on the true purpose behind the use of the word anti-Semitism. He declares that it ''should be eliminated from the English language. 'Anti-Semitism' serves only one purpose today. It is used as a smear word. When so-called Jews feel that anyone opposes any of their objectives they discredit their victims by applying the word 'anti-Semite' or 'anti-Semitic' through all the channels they have at their command and under their control.''

Benjamin Freedman went on to state: *''I can speak with great authority on this subject.* Because so-called Jews were unable to disprove my public statements in 1946 with regard to the situation in Palestine, they spent millions of dollars to smear me as an 'anti-Semite' hoping thereby to discredit me in the eyes of the public who were very interested in what I had to say. Until 1946 I was a 'little saint' to all so-called Jews. *When I disagreed with them publicly on the Zionist intentions in Palestine I became suddenly 'Anti-Semite' #1.*

''It is disgraceful to watch the Christian clergy take up the use of the word 'anti-Semitism.' They should know better. They know that 'anti-Semitism' is a meaningless word in the sense it is used today. They know the correct word is 'Judaeophobe.' *'Anti-Semitism' has developed into the smear word it is today because the word 'Semite' is associated with Christ in the minds of Christians. Christians are accessories to the destruction of the Christian faith by tolerating the use of the smear word 'anti-Semitic' to silence by the most intolerable forms of persecution (employing that smear word) Christians who oppose the evil conspirators''* (Facts Are Facts, p.73).

Jews Speak Out

Interestingly, it is Jewish authors and Jewish organizations which, for the most part, have had the courage to write and speak quite openly on the Jewish issue. Jewish writers such as Arthur Koestler, Haviv Schieber, Alfred Lilienthal, Samuel Roth, Dr. O. J. Graham, Benjamin Freedman, Jack Bernstein and others have done much to open up the Jewish issue to public scrutiny. They are to be applauded for their frankness and intellectual honesty.

73

Their writings (and tapes, Freedman) are highly recommended for those not afraid to face reality.

Other non-Jewish researchers — individuals like Henry Ford, the famed auto maker, Victor Marsden, Pat Brooks, Ted Pike, Gordon Ginn, John L. Bray, Douglas Reed and Eustace Mullins have also toiled courageously to lay basic facts openly before the American public....[1]

Is Jesus Anti-Semitic?

How about Jesus Christ? Is it remotely possible that the One who is "The Way, The Truth and The Life" (John 14:6) could be legitimately charged with being virulently anti-Semitic? In numerous places in the New Testament Jesus opened up with both barrels on the Jewish religious leaders of His day. For example, in Matthew 23 He described them as being full of "hypocrisy and iniquity" (v.13), and of being "serpents" and a "generation of vipers" (v.33). He also condemned them for having turned God's Temple into a "den of thieves" (Luke 19:46).

What Do You Mean, Semite?

As a result of an unrelenting avalanche of Zionist propaganda, the vast majority of Americans have been misled into believing that the word Semite refers almost exclusively to the people who are known as Jews today. In fact, few things could be further from the truth!

Interestingly, the words Semite, Semitism, and anti-Semitism do not even appear in the 1828 edition of Noah's Webster's *American Dictionary of the English Language*. They were invented towards the end of the last century!

According to the highly authoritative *Oxford Universal Dictionary*, 1944, p.1838, the word Semite was first used in 1875. It meant "a person belonging to the race of mankind which includes *most* of the peoples mentioned in Genesis 10 *as descended from Shem* son of Noah, as the *Hebrews, Arabs,* Assyrians, and Arameans. Also a person speaking a Semitic language as his native tongue.'' The same source defines Semitic as ''the attributes characteristic of the Semitic peoples.'' A secondary meaning for Semite, dating from 1885, is given as ''Jewish ideas or influence in politics and society.'' The word anti-Semitism was invented in 1893. This is defined as ''theory, action, or practice directed against the Jews'' (see p.2477).

Langer's Encyclopedia of World History, 1962, p.25, tells us that ''it should always be kept in mind that the term Semite does *not* refer to a race but to a *group of people* speaking Semitic languages (Akkadian, *Hebrew,* Phoenician, Aramaic, *Arabic,* etc).''

Are All Jews Hebrews?

At this juncture another question of critical significance needs to be addressed. Are all those people known as Jews in modern society truly descendants of the ancient Hebrews of Biblical times? Are they the descendants of the people referred to in the Bible as the Children of Israel or Judah? In other words, are they truly Semitic?

Stranger Than Fiction

For many years this writer, having been heavily influenced by a number of world famous radio evangelists, would have answered that question with a resounding, *''Yes!''* He just ''knew'' that it was true. After all, everyone else ''knew'' it to be true! Right? Wrong! For decades he never thought of even questioning his basic assumption! He was *sincere* but he was also sincerely *wrong!*

75

Khazar Jews

It is a basic fact of history that some 90 percent of modern Jewry are *not* of Semitic stock. They (the Khazars) are of Turkish stock. They are descendants of Japheth. As the late Arthur Koestler, a well-known Jewish author, points out, "they came not from Jordan, but from the Volga, not from Canaan, but from the Caucasus... Genetically they were more closely related to the Hun, Uigur and Magyar tribes than to the seed of Abraham, Isaac and Jacob....The story of the Khazar Empire, as it slowly emerges from the past, begins to look like the most cruel hoax that history has ever perpetrated" (*The Thirteenth Tribe,* p.17)....

What Is Judaism?

What is Judaism? Where did it come from? Who controls it? What is its purpose?

The overwhelming majority of Americans — particularly those of the fundamentalist religious persuasion — would answer without hesitation that Judaism is the religious belief system held by Jews from time immemorial. Judaism, they would say, is the religion of the Old Testament and is based solidly on the teachings of Moses. Such an answer might be totally sincere — but it is also totally *wrong!*

Judaism, both in its present form and as it has existed since before the time of Christ, is violently opposed to the God of the Bible.

Shocking? Yes, but true!

Judaism Is Talmudism

"Now Judaism finds its expression in the *Talmud* which is not a remote suggestion and a faint echo thereof, but in which it has become incarnate, in which it has taken form, passing from a state of abstraction into the domain of real things. *The study of Judaism is that of the Talmud, as the study of the Talmud is that of Judaism, as the two are inseparable things, or better, they are the one and the same....* Accordingly, the *Talmud* is the completest expression of religious movement, and this code of endless prescriptions and minute ceremonials represents in its perfection the total work of the religious idea....The miracle was accomplished by a book, the *Talmud*....The *Talmud*, in turn, is composed of two distinct parts, the Mishna and the Gemara; the former the text, the latter the commentary upon the text....

"By the term Mishna we designate a *collection of decisions and traditional laws, embracing all departments of legislation, civil and religious....*This code...is the result of several generations of Rabbis...*nothing indeed can equal the importance of the Talmud, unless it be the ignorance that prevails concerning it...*" *(Talmud,* by Arsene Darmesteter, translated by Henrietta Szold. Quoted in *Facts Are Facts,* pp.63,64).

"The Jewish religion as it is today traces its descent without a break through all the centuries from the Pharisees. Their leading ideas and methods found expression in a literature of enormous extent, of which a great deal is still in existence. *The Talmud is the largest and most important single piece of that literature...and the study of it is essential for any real understanding of Pharisaism*" *(Universal Jewish Encyclopedia,* article on Pharisaism, p.474).

Stop! Read those two quotations again. The information they contain is vital. *Pharisaism. Talmudism. Judaism. They are one and the same!...*

The Rothschilds

No one can deny that over the last two hundred years the Talmudically inspired Khazar Jews have made tremendous strides towards their age-old goal of conquering the world.

Their recent progress is based largely on the spectacular success of the House of Rothschild. Mayer Amschel Bauer, a Khazar or non-Hebrew Jew, was born in Frankfurt, Germany, in 1743. He was the son of Moses Amschel Bauer, an itinerant money lender and goldsmith from Eastern Europe. After working briefly for the Oppenheimer bank in Hanover, Mayer opened a shop or counting house of his own on Judenstrasse (Jew Street) in Frankfurt. Over the door he placed a Red Shield, with a six-pointed-star on it, the emblem of the revolutionary-minded Khazar Jews of Eastern Europe. Shortly thereafter, Mayer Amschel Bauer changed his name to Red Shield, or Rothschild. His business became known as the House of Rothschild.

In 1770 Mayer Rothschild married sixteen year old Gutele Schnaper. They had five sons and five daughters. Their sons were named Amschel, Salomon, Nathan, Kalman (Karl) and Jacob (James).

The Rothschilds were ardent Talmudists. "Even on work days...(Mayer) was apt to take down the big book of the *Talmud* and recite from it... while the entire family must sit stock-still and listen" (*The Rothschilds,* by Frederic Morton, Fawcett Crest, 1961, p.31).

Using flattery and diabolical guile, Mayer Rothschild managed to worm his way into the good graces of Prince William of Hanau, "Europe's most blue-cold blooded loan shark" (p.40). Soon, Rothschild became an agent for this immensely wealthy operator of a "rent-a-mercenary" business. When William was forced to flee to Denmark, he left Rothschild in charge of his wealth. "According to legend, this money was hidden away in wine casks, and, escaping the search of Napoleon's troops when they entered Frankfurt, was restored intact when the elector [William] returned....*The facts are somewhat less romantic, and more businesslike*" (*The Jewish Encyclopedia,* 1905, Vol. 10, p.494).

Yes, the Rothschilds were much "more businesslike"

by Talmudic standards. They embezzled the money from William and used it for their own ends. Among other things, they financed Wellington in his peninsula campaign. *"This was the beginning of the great fortunes of the house"* (p.494).

The Rothschilds *"saw neither peace nor war...neither death nor glory. They saw none of the things that blinded the world. They saw only steppingstones. William had been one. Napoleon would be the next" (The Rothschilds,* pp.38,39). Yes, they saw only opportunities — and people who could be used, and then discarded!

Napoleon Meets His Waterloo

The House of Rothschild's "coup of coups" occurred in 1815 when, with inside information regarding the pending defeat of Napoleon in the Battle of Waterloo, they seized control of the London Stock Exchange. Three years later, they took over France. Europe now lay at their feet. They were now truly *International Bankers.* (For details, see *Descent Into Slavery?* pp. 18-34.)

In the years that followed, the House of Rothschild accumulated vast amounts of money by first setting up, and then financing both sides in numerous wars throughout Europe. The Rothschilds always controlled the "balance of power" in Europe by holding England in the wings until her services were needed to sway any given war in the direction dictated by them. England was always on the winning side!

Rothschilds And America

Rothschild agents were busy in the United States from earliest times. However, it wasn't until the arrival of Jacob Schiff, the son of a rabbi, on the American scene late in the last century that the Rothschilds made dramatic headway towards the economic conquest of America.

Founded On Biblical Principles

From its inception the United States was founded upon LAW, upon Biblical principles. Its government was based upon set standards, just weights and measures. An honest money system was mandated by the Constitution. The dollar was based on *substance* (silver and gold), *not credit.* From the rule of Law came Order, and from Order came Stability. And from Stability came Prosperity! America was the envy of the world. America the Beautiful became the New Promised Land for millions worldwide!

This was basically the national condition at the time of Schiff's arrival from Germany. With no debt and no inflation, America's future looked rosy. The sky was the limit!

Schiff Moves Up

Late in the last century, "the recently established Kuhn, Loeb and Co., bankers, in New York city,...took in the young German immigrant, Jacob Schiff, as partner. *Young Schiff had important financial connections in Europe.* After ten years, Schiff [who had married Loeb's daughter, Teresa] was head of Kuhn, Loeb and Co., Kuhn having died and Loeb retired. Under Schiff's guidance, the house brought European capital into contact with American industry" (*Newsweek,* Feb.1, 1936).

Schiff's "important financial connections" were the Rothschilds! With Rothschild money, Schiff helped finance the activities of John D. Rockefeller (Oil), Edward Harriman (Railroads), Andrew Carnegie (Steel), plus numerous others. He (and the Rothschilds) always ended up with a heavy piece of the action.

As *Truth* magazine stated on December 16, 1912: "Mr. Schiff...represents the Rothschild interests on this side of the Atlantic. He is described as a financial strategist and has been for years the financial minister of the great impersonal power known as Standard Oil.''

Paul Warburg

Early in this century, Schiff was joined on the American scene by another Rothschild ''sharpie'' by the name of Paul Moritz Warburg. Schiff, in his public utterances, began to advocate the creation of a Central Bank. Without one, he said, America was faced with ''the most severe and far reaching money panic in its history.'' *It should be noted that the creation of a central or national bank (''with exclusive monopoly'') is the fifth plank of the Communist Manifesto!*

In 1907, that carefully planned and orchestrated ''panic'' hit the nation. Tens of thousands of innocent people were ruined financially. Schiff and Company made a financial killing!

For the next six years a relentless campaign was waged to convince the American people of the need for a Central Bank. The campaign of deception succeeded. In 1913, the infamous Federal Reserve System was created. Khazar Jew Paul Warburg became its first Chairman.

Upon passage of the Federal Reserve Act in 1913, Congressman Charles Lindbergh stated that the creation of the Fed established ''the most gigantic trust on earth...an invisible government of the monetary power.'' Its passage was ''the worst legislative crime of the ages.'' Senator Henry Cabot Lodge condemned the Fed as being ''in the highest degree menacing to our prosperity...(and) the welfare of the people of the United States.'' Cabot Lodge also prophesied that the creation of the Fed would ''open the way to a vast inflation of the currency (that will) submerge the gold standard in a flood of irredeemable paper currency.''

The Fed, a private corporation, was (and is) owned and

controlled by the Rothschilds and other Khazar Jews. The Rockefellers are the only possibly non-Khazar stockholders.[2]

Khazar Invasion

With control of America's newly created Central Bank — with "exclusive monopoly" — firmly in their grasp, the Khazarian International Bankers lost no time in pursuing additional long range plans already underway.

Congressman Louis T. McFadden, for eleven years chairman of the influential House Committee on Banking and Currency, tells the story: "The money lenders were looking forward to a war between England and Russia and were making preparations for propaganda designed to support England in the United States...Schiff took it upon himself to create a prejudice in the United States against Russia. He did this by presenting the supposed wrongs of the Russian Jews to the American people. Unpleasant tales began to appear in print....By unfair means, a wedge was driven between Russia and the United States.

"One of Schiff's schemes was a sort of wholesale importation of Russian Jews into the United States. He drew up divers and sundry regulations for the temporary transplantation of these Jewish emigrants." Years later "a number of these naturalized Jews returned to Russia. Upon their return to that country, they immediately claimed exemption there from the regulations of domicile imposed on Jews; that is, they claimed the right to live on purely Russian soil because they were American citizens or 'Yankee' Jews. Disorders occurred and were exploited in the American press. Riots and bombings and assassinations, *for which someone furnished money,* took place. *The perpetrators of these outrages appear to have been shielded by powerful financial interests.* While this was going on in Russia, a shameless campaign of lying was conducted here, and large sums of money were spent to make the general American public believe that the Jews in Russia were a simple and guileless folk ground down by the Russians and needing the protection of the great benefactor of the world — Uncle Sam. In other words, we were deceived....The chasm that suddenly opened between ourselves and our old friends and well-wishers in Russia [the real Russians] was a chasm created by Schiff, the vindictive, in his inhuman greed, and he created it in the name of the Jewish religion....Schiff had the 80-year-old treaty of friendship and good will between Russia and the United States denounced" *(Congressional Record,* June 15, 1933. Quoted in *Collective Speeches of Congressman Louis T. McFadden,* pp.390-393). On page 392, McFadden reveals that Schiff and his friends also financed Japan in its 1904-05 war with Russia. The objective was to soften up Russia for the revolution that was being planned for that country. These facts are confirmed in a remarkable article that appeared in the *New York Times,* March 24, 1917, p.1. It may be seen on microfilm in most large libraries.[3]

The Jewish planned, led and financed revolutions in Russia (unsuccessful in 1905-06, and successful in 1917) resulted in a massive expansion of Jewish (Khazar) power and influence worldwide.

Winston Churchill And The Bolshevik Revolution

The statement that the Bolshevik Revolution in 1917 was ''Jewish planned, led and financed'' will probably sound outrageous to many. After all, ''we don't read that in our history books and in our school and college textbooks, so it can't be true.''

The simple truth, however, is that the real history of the Russian Revolution has long since been buried under an avalanche of lies. The truth has been blacked out. What we read in our history and text books is a deliberate fabrication.

The basic facts were laid out in graphic detail by none other than Winston Churchill. In a 1920 magazine article, Churchill focused in on ''the schemes of the International Jews (who have) divorced from their minds all spiritual hopes of the next world.'' He then zeroed in on their plot to create a One World Government: *''This movement among the Jews is not new.* From the days of Spartacus-Weishaupt [the founder of the Illuminati in 1776], to those of Karl Marx, and down to Trotsky (Russia), Bela Kuhn (Hungary), Rosa Luxembourg (Germany), and Emma Goldman (United States), *this worldwide conspiracy for the overthrow of civilization and for the reconstruction of society on the basis of arrested development, of envious malevolence, and impossible equality,* has been steadily growing. It played...a definitely recognizable part in the tragedy of the French Revolution. *It has been the mainspring of every subversive movement during the nineteenth century;* and now at last *this band of extraordinary personalities from the underworld of the great cities of Europe and America* have gripped the Russian people by the hair of their heads, and have become practically the undisputed masters of that enormous empire.

Terrorist Jews

''There is no need to exaggerate the part played in the creation of Bolshevism and in the actual bringing about of the Russian Revolution by these international and for the most part atheistical Jews. It is certainly a very great one; it probably outweighs all others. With the notable exception of Lenin, *the majority of the leading figures are Jews. Moreover, the principal inspiration and driving force comes from the Jewish leaders....*

''In the Soviet institutions the preponderance of Jews...is astonishing. And the prominent, if not indeed the principal, part in the *system of terrorism* applied by the Ex-

84

traordinary Commission for Combatting Counter Revolution has been taken by Jews, and in some notable cases by Jewesses. The same evil predominance was obtained by Jews in the brief period of terror during which Bela Kuhn ruled in Hungary. The same phenomenon has been presented in Germany (especially in Bavaria), so far as this madness has been allowed to prey upon the temporary prostration of the German people. Although in all these countries there are many non-Jews every whit as bad as the worst of the Jewish revolutionaries, the part played by the latter in proportion to their numbers in the population is astonishing....

"The fact that in many cases Jewish interests and Jewish places of worship are excepted by the Bolsheviks from their universal hostility has tended more and more to associate the Jewish race in Russia with the villainies which are now being perpetrated" *(Illustrated Sunday Herald,* February 20, 1920, p.5).[4]

Read now the clear and unmistakable statements of Jewish writers: "There is much in the fact that so many Jews are Bolsheviks. *The ideals of Bolshevism [the philosophy which motivates it] are consonant with many of the highest ideals of Judaism" (Jewish Chronicle,* London, April 4, 1919). Or, as Rabbi Stephen Wise admitted some years later: "Some call it Marxism. I call it Judaism" (*The American Bulletin,* May 15, 1935). And, from yet another source: *"It is not an accident that Judaism gave birth to Marxism,* and it is not an accident that the Jews readily took up Marxism. *All this is in perfect accord with the progress of Judaism and the Jews"* (*A Program for the Jews and an Answer to All Anti-Semites,* by Harry Waton, p.148. Published 1939). In a newspaper interview, Jacob Schiff's grandson, John, estimated that "the old man sank about $20,000,000 (1917 dollars!) for the final triumph of Bolshevism in Russia" (*New York Journal American,* February 3, 1949).

History records that up to 83,000,000 (eighty-three

85

million) innocent Russians (many of them Christians) were butchered by this malevolent system of terror and destruction *(The Time of Stalin: Portrait of a Tyranny,* by Anton Antonov-Ovseyenko). The Holocaust lasted from 1917 to 1953. It is perfectly understandable why certain people in the United States would wish to conveniently "forget" such facts!

Anti-Semitism was officially outlawed in Russia following the Khazarian takeover! Anti-Communism was considered anti-Semitism. The penalty for anti-Semitism was death! *(Encyclopedia Judaica,* p.798).

Khazar Jews In America

As biographer Frederic Morton points out, the Rothschilds always operate under "an umbrella of silence....*In the best circles one does not make history by the sweat of one's own brow. One hires the makers" (The Rothschilds,* p.125).

One such "hireling" was Woodrow Wilson (*Challenging Years,* p.161). Yes, Wilson was guided and directed by "very different personages from what (was) imagined by those who (were) not behind the scenes" (*Coningsby,* by Benjamin Disraeli, p.233).

Woodrow Wilson was a puppet of the International Bankers. It was he who signed into law the Federal Reserve Act *(The fifth plank of the Communist Manifesto)* within minutes of its passage by a sorely depleted Congress on December 23, 1913. It was Wilson who, following his re-election in 1916 under the slogan, "He kept us out of war," asked Congress to declare war on Germany. Congress complied. It was also Wilson who signed into law the illegally ratified 16th Amendment — the income tax amendment — in 1916![5] *A "heavy progressive or graduated income tax" is the second plank in the Communist Manifesto!*

Among President Wilson's top advisers were Col. E. Mandell House, the son of a top Rothschild agent; Bernard

86

Baruch, a Jewish Wall Street manipulator; and Rabbi Stephen Wise.

What "hold" did these men have over Wilson? During his term as President of Princeton, Wilson was alleged to have had an affair with Mrs. Mary Allen Hulbert Peck. He wrote her letters which are said to have been purchased by Bernard Baruch for $65,000 (*Scandals In the Highest Office,* by Hope R. Miller, Random House, 1973, p.196).

Amid howls of protest, Wilson also appointed Louis D. Brandeis, a "leader of the Zionist cause," to the Supreme Court. Declares Rabbi Stephen Wise: *"From the very beginning...Brandeis and I knew that in Wilson we had and would always have outstanding sympathy for the Zionist program and purpose"* (*Challenging Years,* pp.186,187).

Following his appointment to the Supreme Court, Brandeis "did not cease to stand out as...*a leader of the forces of liberalism"* (pp.186,200).

For services rendered, Woodrow Wilson was awarded the 1919 Nobel Peace Prize!

Socialism Is Jewish

Both socialism and communism (based on humanism, the belief that collective man, as manifested in the state, is god) are Jewish in nature. Both sprang from the same source, and have the same objective! In the words of the *Universal Jewish Encyclopedia,* they are manifestations of "Jewish Messianic feeling..." (p.584). See also *Jewish Encyclopedia,* p.420.

Socialism At Work

From its blood-drenched beginnings (1917), Communist Russia (the Union of Soviet *Socialist* Republics) has been a social and economic disaster. Even for Russia to survive at a subsistence level, it has been necessary for the

Red regime to be propped up by constant infusions of capital and technology from the West.

Former U.S. Secretary of the Treasury William E. Simon, himself a Jew, puts the Russian situation in its proper perspective: ''Suppose you ask a bank for a loan and said: I want an interest rate well below what you charge your best customers. I don't want to make any payments on the principal for the next six years. I won't give you anything for security. And, of course, I will use the money for any purpose I please.

''The banker doubtless would laugh, for no American home-owner, businessman or corporation, not even the American government, can borrow money on such terms. But the Soviet Union can...'' (*Reader's Digest,* September 1988).

Interestingly, Mr. Simon never mentioned the fact that, as a government official, he endorsed such activities.

Even with $130,000,000,000 in low-interest, unsecured loans from the West, the economy of ''the evil empire,'' allegedly our #1 Enemy, is disintegrating at an alarming rate. It is on the verge of collapse. Socialism has proven a catastrophic failure!

Since it was first recognized politically, and bailed out economically, by the Roosevelt administration in 1933, the Soviet Union has never been a threat to the United States or the Western world. It has never been anything more than a pawn in the con game being played on the world by the Khazarian International Bankers.[6]

Socialism In America

Socialism, the Jewish ''Messiah'' *(Universal Jewish Encyclopedia,* p.584), made little headway in America's Christian Republic prior to the advent of Franklin D. Roosevelt in 1933. Since that time, with the able assistance of the best politicians that money can buy, plus an unending propaganda blitz by the Jewish-controlled television industry, the Jewish-controlled movie industry, and the Jewish-controlled publishing industry, the people of the United States have been led steadily down the primrose path towards their destruction and slavery. It has been seduction through lying propaganda!

I can hear screams of protest in reaction to each of the above statements. In the minds of many, this writer has probably "flipped his lid" and "gone completely overboard" by saying that the media in America is Jewish-controlled. Such statements are ridiculous and absurd. Right? Wrong!

Each of the above statements is absolutely accurate. Each is thoroughly documented. Check it out for yourself!

MOVIES: "From the early days of motion pictures, Jews have played a major role in the development of the industry, and have been prominent in all its branches...all the large Hollywood companies...were founded and controlled by Jews. In addition, the first bank to finance the film industry was the Jewish-owned Kuhn, Loeb and Co., in 1919" (*Encyclopedia Judaica,* article on Motion Pictures, p.446).

TELEVISION: "In the U.S. Jews have played a major role in the development of television and radio....They have been well represented in all executive and technical aspects of the industry....Jews held key positions in the emergence and shaping of all three major U.S. networks. David Sarnoff started the National Broadcasting Company (NBC) in 1926...Columbia Broadcasting Service (CBS) was founded under the presidency of William S. Paley...(and at) the third network, the American Broadcasting Company (ABC), Leonard Goldenson became its president. Apart from the heads of the major networks, many Jews worked at all levels of the organizations as well as in the smaller networks, educational services, local stations, etc." (*Encyclopedia Judaica,* article on Television and Radio).

PUBLISHING: The *Judaica* list of Jewish-controlled

publishing houses is much too long to print in full. Among those listed are Viking, Knopf, Random House, Simon and Schuster, and Harcourt Brace and Co. Nahum Goldman, writing in *Dispersion and Unity,* p. 11, Jerusalem, 1972, stated: "Most of the American literary scene is today predominantly Jewish...."

Khazar Bankers

The Khazar bankers and their treacherous American accomplices, through a multitude of deceptions (a long series of wars, giveaway programs at home and abroad, confiscatory taxation and ever-increasing government regulations) have stripped Americans of their God-given freedoms and wealth and made them paupers in their own land.

Following the Socialist road map supplied by the Jewish Messiah has placed us nearly $3,000,000,000,000 (three trillion dollars) in debt. Naturally, most of the interest *(usury)* on that imagination-defying amount, currently estimated at $150,000,000,000 annually, is being paid to, you guessed it, Rothschild and Company — the International Bankers!

Debt is Slavery. It prevents the government from governing in any real sense. As in any similar situation, the borrower is always subject to the dictates of the lender. The lender calls the tune. And the borrower dances to that tune!

"The Usurer loves the borrower, as the Ivy loves the Oak: The Ivy loves the Oak to grow up by it, so the Usurer loves the borrower to grow rich by him. The Ivy clasps the Oak like a lover, but it clasps out all the juice and sap, that the Oak cannot thrive after: So the Usurer lends like a friend, but he covenants like an enemy, for he clasps the borrower with such bands, that ever after he diminishes as fast as the other increases" (Henry Smith, a Puritan preacher, 1591. Quoted in *Usury: Destroyer of Nations,* by S.C. Mooney, p.232).

America pays the Khazar Jew bankers tribute. It

"The Usurer Loves the Borrower as the Ivy Loves the Oak?"

actually rises in the morning to earn its living by utilizing credit issued by the Khazar bankers, and occupies its days in making money to pay them interest, which is to make them even wealthier. It goes to bed at night owing them hundreds of millions of dollars more than when it arose only hours before.

Under Socialism, the Jewish Messiah, even most two pay-check families are struggling desperately to make ends meet. Many are deeply in debt.

America is presently the world's greatest debtor nation. We owe more than all other nations combined.

The Rothschilds have even gone so far as to place their powerful occult emblem, the six-pointed-star, on the reverse side of their worthless, irredeemable $1 Federal Reserve Notes. This abomination is seen hovering, like a vulture, over the American Eagle. On the left (!) side may be seen the infamous Illuminati pyramid, advertising *Novus Ordo Seclorum,* the satanically-inspired New World Order![7]

Hollywood's War On Christianity

For many years Hollywood has been engaged in a war against Christianity. At first the anti-Christ sentiment was strictly covert. It was carefully concealed in slick, carefully inserted innuendos designed to undermine Christian truths, patriotism, the family, law and order and other basic values. In similar manner socialism, humanism, and situation ethics were extolled and promoted. The national foundation of morality was steadily undermined. It began to slowly crumble.

With the passage of time Hollywood's assault on Christianity — and, ultimately, the Person of Jesus Christ Himself — became increasingly brazen. Hollywood embraced and extolled immorality, sexual perversion, and virtually every other type of moral aberration. To condemn such acts would, we were told, be bigoted, narrow minded, and self-righteous. We must, after all, be sensitive, sympathetic and understanding.

But *not* with Christians! Not with those who worship the Sovereign God and confess Jesus Christ as Lord and Savior! Not with those who believe in and practice love, truth, morality, and integrity as a way of life! Not for those who stand for personal responsibility and law and order! No way! Such people are only worthy of contempt, ridicule and slander.

The Last Temptation

The 1988 release of the film *The Last Temptation of Christ* — the very embodiment of the vicious spirit of anti-Christ which permeates Hollywood — was the natural outgrowth of Hollywood's ever-increasing campaign of slander and ridicule against both Christianity and traditional values.

As Patrick J. Buchanan observed in his nationally syndicated column, "the movie represents an act of cinematic vandalism against the beliefs that Christians hold sacred: it is a deliberate profanation of the faith." *Last Temptations* "is a salacious, sleazy stunt...a stunt manifesting a contemptuous disregard for the injury (of) devout Christians....

"Christians, however, *America's unfashionable majority*, may be mocked; their preachers may be parodied in books and on film; their faith may be portrayed as superstitious folly. And secular society, invoking the First Amendment, will rush to the defense of the defamers, not the defamed.

"The battle over *Last Temptation* is one more skirmish in the century's struggle over whose values, whose beliefs shall be exalted in American culture, and whose may be derided and disparaged.

"What all of Hollywood...is saying with its unqualified endorsement of *The Last Temptation of Christ* is: 'Hey, you Christians, look here; we're showing your God and your Savior, Jesus Christ, having sex with Mary

Magdalene, *now, what are you going to do about it?*'''' (*Daily News,* Los Angeles, July 27, 1988).

A good question! What are you going to do about it?

Buchanan also observed that ''we live in an age where the ridicule of blacks is forbidden, where anti-Semitism is punishable by political death, but where Christian-bashing is a popular indoor sport; and films mocking Jesus Christ are considered avant-garde.''

No Great Surprise

In the light of the thoroughly documented and irrefutable facts contained in this book, it should come as no great surprise that a Jewish-controlled movie studio would willingly and, indeed, willfully, produce and distribute a vile and vicious cinematic abomination such as *The Last Temptation of Christ.* Among the Khazar Jews who run MCA-Universal are: Lew Wasserman, MCA Chairman of the Board; Sidney Sheinberg, MCA President; Gary Goldstein, National Promotions and Field Operations, and Simon Kornblitt, Vice President of Marketing. As Martin Luther would put it, ''they excruciatingly blaspheme our Lord Jesus Christ.'' *In other words, this movie is a direct assault upon the Biblical revelation of Jesus Christ.*

As might be expected, the only nationwide cinema chain willing to exhibit this anti-Christ abomination was the Jewish-owned and controlled Cineplex-Odeon Theaters. Its president is Garth Drabinsky. Cineplex-Odeon is part of the Seagram-Bronfman empire. The Bronfmans are a Canadian family whose immense whiskey fortune may be traced to the days of Prohibition. Historically, they have funded Jewish causes (*Encyclopedia Judaica,* article on Bronfman).

(This chapter was excerpted from *Anti-Semitism And The Babylonian Connection,* available from Emissary Publications, 9205 SE Clackamas Rd., Clackamas, OR 97015. $6.40 postpaid.)

CHAPTER SEVEN

THE COST OF TRUE FREEDOM

Everywhere today the merchants of fear are peddling their wares. Their goal is very simple: to create an inner terror in their serfs which compels them to deny all principles and even God Himself rather than offend those holding the reins of power. Satan is weaving this web.

Can you imagine the deluded Evil One looking on earth as one giant chess board? He moves his kings to destroy his pawns, for he knows his time is short. His only vengeance against the Almighty is to take as many lost souls down to hell with him as he can.

Satan's army thus consists of Establishment figures who have won their wealth and power by selling their souls, and the pawns or serfs who treasure their necks, their reputations, or their sources of income over their souls.

Satan's fatal error in his madness is that he sees all mankind on that chessboard. He has always refused to acknowledge the total victory of the Lord Jesus Christ on Calvary, shown in His glorious Resurrection. The Evil One cannot bear the awful reality of the elect, the redeemed — God's army here on earth! That there are those who have been set free by faith in the shed Blood of the Son of God from this chess game — no, that cannot be! That these saints have not denied their Lord Jesus over the ages and will not, in the days to come — bah, humbug! Every man has his price, according to the devil!

That is why tribulation must come. Almighty God will

prove to all His creation that His power is sufficient to keep His own true to Him in a hostile world.

One fact professing Christians seem to miss in the error-laden visible church of our day is that *God is Sovereign*. He created Lucifer, the shining one or "son of the dawn," fully knowing that this anointed cherub would fall, be filled with pride, and become Satan (Isaiah 14:12-14, and Ezekiel 28:11-19). He could have stamped out the adversary as soon as he fell, as one would crush an ant. But He did not. For God wanted a family of children, not a factory of robots programmed with computers.

The clear, unpopular teaching of Scripture is that God has allowed the existence of Satan to test mankind. *Many* claim to love the Almighty, and believe in His Son, Jesus Christ. However, talk is cheap. God must allow the tests of life and our momentous times to reveal who are truly His.

"And the Lord said unto Satan, Hast thou considered my servant Job, that there is none like him in the earth, a perfect and an upright man, one that feareth God and escheweth evil?

"Then Satan answered the LORD and said, Doth Job fear God for nought? Hast thou not made a hedge about him, and about his house, and about all that he hath on every side? Hast thou blessed the works of his hands, and his substance is increased in the land. But put forth thine hand now, and touch all that he hath, and he will curse thee to thy face."[1]

A careful study of the book of Job will show that God gave *permission* to Satan to test Job's loyalty to the Almighty, even defining the parameters of the testing, in each case. Did Job ever curse God, even when urged by his foolish wife to do so?

"The LORD gave, and the LORD hath taken away; blessed be the name of the LORD."[2] Do these sound like the words of an apostate rebel against God?

Job did indeed know God. However, after the *testing,* that knowledge had permeated his heart as well as his head. Then he could say, "I have heard of thee by the hearing of the ear: but now mine eyes seeth thee."[3]

Is that not what every believer longs for — to truly see our Lord God? Remember Philip's impulsive cry? "Lord, show us the Father, and it is enough for us!"[4]

Yet that request came immediately after the Lord Jesus had said, "I am the way, the truth, and the life; no one comes to the Father, but by me."[5]

Decades ago when my husband and I trained for missionary service at Columbia Bible College, then-President J. Allen Fleece gave the following analysis of that verse, John 14:6:

"Jesus is not saying He is three qualities: way, plus truth, plus life. No, He is saying He alone is the Way: Truth plus Life — the Eternal Word plus His Life-giving Spirit!"

Dr. Fleece went on to say that the Lord Jesus, Second Person of the Triune Godhead, is the *Logos,* the Living Word, while the Bible is His written Word. Both agree, without exception, for the latter is God-breathed by the Spirit of the former.

The great Bible teacher also warned that the written Word without the Spirit is dead orthodoxy. Truth plus life makes up the Lord Jesus' Way! (Please do not confuse the Way, God's Son, with the cult, "The Way International" — a satanic counterfeit!)

Years later I heard a British preacher, ex-gypsy John Barr, say the same thing in a slightly different way: "The Word without the Spirit? You dry up. The Spirit without the Word? You blow up. The Spirit and the Word? You grow up!"

We shall see God prove that to His church as never before in this final decade of the 20th Century and dawn of the 21st Century. Prophetic voices as diverse as Billy

Graham, James McKeever, and Rick Joyner are predicting great persecution of true believers worldwide, now.

How uncanny are the words of that giant among prophets, Daniel, in such a time! ''And such as do wickedly against the covenant shall he corrupt by flatteries: but the people that do know their God shall be strong and do exploits. And they that understand among the people shall instruct many: yet they shall fall by the sword, and by flame, by captivity, and by spoil, many days.''[6]

That last clause is almost always left out of messages on these verses. Why? Because there is something in us which resists God's call to the martyrs. Never mind that the Greek *martus* (witness, as in Acts 1:8) and *martur* (martyr, as in Acts 22:20) are from the same root. The flesh does not want to suffer! Perhaps that is why we hear so little of verses like these:

''You have not resisted unto blood, striving against sin.''[7]

''Remember the word that I said unto you, The servant is not greater than his lord. If they have persecuted me, they will also persecute you; if they have kept my sayings, they will keep yours also.''[8]

''These things have I spoken unto you, that you should not be offended. They shall put you out of the synagogues: yea, the time cometh, that whosoever killeth you will think that he doeth God service. And these things will they do unto you because they have not known the Father, nor me.''[9]

In the first three chapters of the book of Revelation the glorified Lord Jesus Christ had messages for seven bodies of believers in Asia Minor. To most He had words of both warning and praise, and to all He gave promises to the overcomers among them. Yet two groups, Smyrna and Philadelphia, received no rebuke, only encouragement. Oddly enough, they had both suffered greatly at the hands of the same people. Hear God's Word to them and to us called to be the non-celebrity Jeremiahs, Deborahs, Stephens, Lydias, John Alan Coeys, and Haviv Schiebers of our day:

"I know thy works, and tribulation, and poverty (but thou art rich), and I know the blasphemy of them which say they are Jews, and are not, but are the synagogue of Satan. Fear none of those things which thou shall suffer: behold, the devil shall cast some of you into prison, that you may be tried; and you shall have tribulation ten days; be thou faithful unto death, and I will give thee a crown of life. He that hath an ear, let him hear what the Spirit saith unto the churches. He that overcometh shall not be hurt of the second death."[10]

"Behold, I will make them of the synagogue of Satan, which say they are Jews, and are not, but do lie; behold, I will make them to come and worship before thy feet, and to know that I have loved thee. Because thou hast kept the word of my patience, I also will keep thee from the hour of temptation, which shall come upon the whole world, to try them that dwell upon the earth. Behold, I come quickly: hold that fast which thou hast, that no man take thy crown. Him that overcometh will I make a pillar in the temple of my God, and he shall go out no more: and I will write upon him the name of my God, and the name of the city of my God, which is the New Jerusalem, which cometh down out of heaven from my God: and I will write upon him my new name. He that hath an ear, let him hear what the Spirit saith unto the churches."[11]

War clouds loom above us. *How* is the church to *hear* what the Spirit is saying to the churches, today? Over three decades of experience as God's child and His servant have taught me to trust His written Word, the Bible. It is still and will always be "the only infallible rule of faith and practice," as 1100 Puritan and Presbyterian Bible scholars determined in the Westminster Confession of 1643. For well over three decades I have tried to read God's Word through once a year, in its entirety. The system I use is in the appendix of this book, as is the Westminster Confession Shorter Catechism. Do study it!

Years ago the biography and autobiography of 19th-Century saint George Mueller gave me direction for that early morning quiet time with God. Read the Word first; then praise God and seek Him in prayer. Be prepared to *spend time* with God. It usually takes at least half an hour even to let "the things of the world grow strangely dim," in the words of the old hymn, "Turn Your Eyes Upon Jesus." An hour is better; two hours are better still. Let no one delude himself into thinking he can snap his fingers at Almighty God and get an answer from Him without abiding in His presence.

Now, having said all that, let us be intensely practical. I can read my daily chapters in Leviticus, or Psalms, or Jeremiah, or Matthew, or Ephesians — and still not be sure of *everything* I should do, whom I should see, or where I should go, that day. This is where faith comes in, and the work of the Holy Spirit. If I put my life, my day, my family, and my work in His hands, I can trust Him that even some "interruptions" may be His perfect will for that day. Having prayed, sought direction, interceded for others, and bound the powers of darkness in the Name of Jesus Christ in agreement, my husband and I go forward in confidence that God will work His will through us and our family that day. (My handbook on spiritual warfare, *Healing of the Mind,* teaches how to cut off demonic harassment and hindrance. A detailed description here is beyond the scope of this brief book.)

Then there are the disciplines of Christian fasting, giving, and forgiving, dealt with in my book, *A Call To War.* A second book, *Prayer Power,* reprinted in the same volume as that one, tells how to mobilize prayer warriors for effective warfare, intercession, travail, and Christian reconstruction. To duplicate that work here is also impossible.

We recommend them and *The Return of the Puritans,* my fifth book, for all who sense God's call on their lives for effective prayer and fasting in these momentous times. "Things go better with prayer" is more than a motto; it is a reality. In fact, "Never do more than you can afford to saturate with prayer," said Elmer Thompson, founder of *World Team Mission.* This is excellent advice for every believer. The devil will ever try to distract from the best with the good, which is why we must purpose in our hearts to put God *first* in our hearts, in our stewardship of time and money, and all other priorities.

While we are on this subject, I recommend *Daughters of the King,* for those of my own sex. In its recent edition I have added a study guide with Scriptures and discussion questions suitable for Bible studies, prayer or sharing groups. The book is for "liberated women — not women's libbers!" It deals with godly femininity, hopefully blasting the feminist argument out of the water.

Let no one be so naive as to think that feminism is dead. Even in Christian circles there are those who want to have their mail sent to them as "Ms.," call themselves "prochoice," or push "egalitarian marriage" where there is no captain on the ship, only a competing pair of "executive officers"!

What kind of fruit has this Leftist tree produced? The breakdown of the family, for starters. Once the family is gone, civilization is gone. "Things fall apart; the center cannot hold." In that chaos, freedom becomes irrelevant.

My godly mother taught me years ago the difference between liberty and license. She asked me to flail my arms around, which I did.

"That is freedom, or liberty," she said. "Now close your eyes and do the same thing."

I did, not realizing that she had stepped right up next to me. Of course, my arm hit her. Startled, I opened my eyes and apologized.

101

"That is license," she said. "We are only free to act in a way that will not harm others. Once we begin to hurt others with our words or other choices, we have broken the royal law of Scripture: "Thou shalt love thy neighbor as thyself.""

My husband and I have been active in the freedom movement to see America survive as a Christian Republic since 1974. In that time we have seen many patriots who are not Christians and Christians who are not patriots. Both groups are in terrible danger, for they are building their life foundations on sand.

In the first group, unconverted patriots are willing to die for America (or Canada, or England, or Germany, whatever their national home). But if they did, they would wake up in hell! John 3:1-19 are still in the Book, along with Numbers 21:4-9, Acts 4:12, Romans 3:23 and 6:23. No works of our own will ever get us adopted in the Family of God: only what the Lord Jesus Christ did on Calvary, dying for our sins, later rising from the dead. That is the gospel, the good news for the starving, spiritually dead population of this planet — all five billion-plus of them.

In the second group, deluded professing Christians believe they can move through life like the three monkeys: "See no evil, hear no evil, speak no evil." They are willing to "accept Christ" and His salvation for themselves, and perhaps even witness to others and support missions. But function as salt (preservative and purifier)? Never! The excuses one hears most often from such people is "God has not called me to that," or "It doesn't matter what happens to the country, because I won't be here!"

Neither excuse holds any water at all. The "God-has-not-called-me-to-that" bunch have never read the following Scriptures, apparently. (Or perhaps they have read them "dispensationally" — that is, not for today!)

"Curse ye Meroz, said the angel of the LORD, curse

102

ye bitterly the inhabitants thereof; because they came not to the help of the LORD, to the help of the LORD against the mighty.''[12]

"And the LORD said unto him, Go through the midst of the city, through the midst of Jerusalem, and set a mark upon the foreheads of the men that sigh and that cry for all the abominations that be done in the midst thereof. And to the others he said in mine hearing, Go ye after him through the city, and smite: let not your eye spare, neither have ye pity: Slay utterly the young and the old, both maids and little children, and women; but come not near any man upon whom is the mark; and begin at my sanctuary.''[13]

"My people are destroyed for lack of knowledge: because thou hast rejected knowledge, I will also reject thee, that thou shalt be no priest to me: seeing thou hast forgotten the law of thy God, I will also forget your children.''[14]

"Who will rise up for me against the evil doers? Or who will stand up for me against the workers of iniquity?''[15]

"And I sought for a man among them, that should make up the hedge, and stand in the gap before me for the land, that I should not destroy it: but I found none.''[16]

"Yea, truth faileth; and he that departeth from evil maketh himself a prey: and the LORD saw it, and it displeased him that there was no judgment. And he saw that there was no man, and wondered that there was no intercessor...''[17]

"Ye are the salt of the earth: but if the salt have lost his savour, wherewith shall it be salted? It is thenceforth good for nothing, but to be cast out, and to be trodden under foot of men.''[18]

We could go on and on like this. But is it necessary? Are we like the mule that the old farmer had to hit with a two-by-four to "get his attention"?

Since God has laid a sense of urgency upon my heart about the message of this book, impressing me that it is to be a "quick-read," let us pause and consider the above; then come to some conclusions.

God is clearly looking for those who will stand with Him and for Him in the gap against the evil doers. He is looking for intercessors, teachers, businessmen, servicemen, farmers, plumbers, electricians, homemakers, statesmen, teenagers and even children whom He can have his angels mark for protection before He sends awesome judgments on the land. He wants a remnant who can be used of Him to rebuild in righteousness on the ruins and rubble left from the destruction of the fall of "Babylon the Great" and this world system.

The Lord Jesus never *asked* us to be salt; He simply stated that we are. He called it like it is when He warned about the penalty for losing our "saltness," or the concern to preserve and purify those around us. He said we shall be outcasts, exiles "trodden under feet of men." Folks, that means slavery. Which will you be: salt? or slaves?

At about this time, the *second* dispensational delusion is probably kicking up in some minds: "What does it matter? *I won't be here!*" Friend, you have been taken, conned. There never will be any pre-tribulation "rapture" or catching up to be with the Lord Jesus before trouble here in the West, despite what clever lawyers John Darby and C.I. Scofield have said on the subject. God does not love you or me more than He loved the 62 million Chinese the Reds killed in the 1940s or the 83 million the Bolsheviks and Soviets killed over a period of several decades in the USSR. Many of those were Christians, faithful unto death, who have now received the crown of life, just as John Alan Coey did in Rhodesia in 1975 and countless other soldiers of the cross, over the ages.

One of the favorite comments of the late Jim Elliot, martyred by the Auca Indians of South America as he tried to reach them with the gospel, was this: "He is no fool who gives what he cannot keep to gain what he cannot lose!"[19]

The Lord Jesus put it this way: "If any man will come after me, let him deny himself, and take up his cross daily, and follow me. For whosoever will save his life shall lose it: but whosoever will lose his life for my sake, the same shall save it" (Luke 9:23-24).

It is a matter of indifference to me and most of God's servants whether we are to be part of the remnant people God is raising up in this day, or to win the martyr's crown. We shall leave that decision to the Sovereign God. However, it seems obvious that the same kind of preparation is necessary for all of us in both groups, if we are to hear His, "well done, thou good and faithful servant."

The Lord Jesus gave three priorities for His servants who were to be true to Him in the evil day, and be ready for an accounting with Him on His return. They are *watch, pray* and *occupy.* Three acrostics serve as reminders on those words, which can be written on the fly-leaf of our Bibles and shared with others whom we shall be teaching His ways:

W — Wait on God daily, in the Word and in praise and prayer, for His directions for that day (Isaiah 40:31).

A — Advance Biblical righteousness by learning truth and taking a stand for God where His will is being challenged (John 8:31,32, and Ephesians 6:10-18).

T — Teach others truth: to know Jesus Christ and the authority in His Name; to be filled with His Spirit, and be strong in Him (Acts 1:8; II Timothy 2:1-3; Matthew 28:18-20).

C — Call the shots on evil and error, but do not attack people (I Corinthians 2:15; Matthew 7:1-6).

H — Heed the signs of the times, accepting the Lord's challenge to give at least as much attention to them as the weather report! (Matthew 16:2,3).

To do the latter requires getting "free press" material in order to know what is going on in our country and world. As we have seen in the last chapter, the major media are controlled by antichrist forces who are at war with our God and His people. Here are the sources we recommend:

Weeklies:

Christian News, Box 168, New Haven, MO 63068 ($15 per year).

WORLD, Box 2330, Asheville, NC 28802 ($22 per year).

Spotlight, 300 Independence Avenue, S.E., Washington, DC 20003 (Populist, not evangelical like the above two; $30 per year).

Monthlies:

AFA Journal, Drawer 2440, Tupelo, MS 38803 ($15 per year).

The National Educator, P.O. Box 333, Fullerton, CA 92632 ($15 per year; carries my column).

Plymouth Rock Foundation *FAC Sheet,* Box 577, Marlborough, NH 03455 (donation basis).

The Mantooth Report, Route 1, Box 387, Salem, IN 47167 ($12 per year).

The Last Trumpet, Box 806, Beaver Dam, WI 53916 (donation basis).

Upright Ostrich, Box 11691, Milwaukee, WI 53211 ($25 per year).

The Moneychanger, P.O. Box 341753, Memphis, TN 38184 ($65 per year).

Bi-Monthly:

Midnight Messenger, 9205 SE Clackamas Road, Clackamas, OR 97015 ($24, 12 issues). Carries the writings of Des Griffin, plus numerous others.

We get all of the above, and would not be without them. There are other fine publications, but each of these has some unique quality not found in any others. For example, *The Last Trumpet* is written by a pastor who was in witchcraft for years before his conversion to Christ. He explains the occult significance of moves "The Establishment" make, with suggestions for prayer.

The National Educator, Jim Townsend's powerful

monthly, includes my column. This is how I am able to update our intercessors. Those interested in committing one day a week to fasting and a half-hour at least, daily, to prayer for a Great Awakening and the restoration of our Christian Republic should drop me a postcard (Box 1212, Fairview, NC 28730). The way we recommend you pray is in the acrostic that follows, and tract, *A Chain of Prayer,* reprinted in the Appendix.

P — Persist in daily prayer, as the prayer parable teaches (Luke 18:1-8).

R — Repent of all sin in your life, for God to hear you (Isaiah 59:1, 2 and Proverbs 28:9).

A — "Avenge us of our adversary," content for victory prayer (Luke 18:3, 7, 8).

Y — Yield to the Lordship of Jesus Christ; obey Him! (Luke 6:46; Matthew 7:13-27).

Most of what we have dealt with so far in this chapter is in getting our own priorities straight, in total surrender to our risen Lord Jesus Christ. However, we are not to be simply sponges, soaking up truth. No, we are to be the fountains or at least pipelines of God's life to others, passing on both Biblical and informational truth to those about us.

How do we do this?

Over the years we at NPL have discovered that God lays upon the hearts of many of His children to inform others. Most people around us have no basis on which to even *understand* the free press material just recommended, much less long to get it. Therefore, we provide foundational material for dedicated colporteurs (i.e., distributors of Christian Bibles and books who are simply individuals whom God has apparently called to do this). No offer we have ever made available equals our "10/10 offer" advertised after the appendix of this book. Its ten books challenge and teach spiritually as well as inform on both the Christian history of America and Red attempt to destroy her. We recommend every family of believers have these books, read them, and pass them on to others. Furthermore, for all who order them, we shall allow you to take *40% off from now on (bookstore discount) for all orders $40 retail or more from NPL.* If you order $100 retail or more, you may take 50% off. In either case, add 10% shipping after arriving at the discounted figure.

There is no time to lose. To that end, here is the final acrostic to help us prepare for the momentous times that are coming — on the word "occupy."

O — Out of debt; try to sell what you cannot pay off (Romans 13:8 and Proverbs 22:7).

C — Chains of prayer formed, as the tract in the appendix advises (Ezekiel 7:23).

C — Change your living habits to maximum simplicity (Matthew 6:24-34; II Timothy 2:4).

U — Use time and money for your "Noah-functions": to get out truth, and prepare for the survival of your family and those of God's family He may send your way (Matthew 24:45,46; Hebrews 11:7; II Peter 2:5).

P — Patronize privately owned free enterprise, especially of fellow-believers, even by barter when we may be shut out of the market place (Revelation 13, especially verses 16 and 17).

Y — Yeast principle: spread truth where it can grow (Matthew 7:6, and 10:16). Yeast grows only in the right temperature: not too hot; not too cold.

A careful study of the "OCCUPY" acrostic will reveal that economic warfare is one of our greatest weapons. The god mammon must be dethroned not only in thoughts, but also in actions. Buy and barter power must also be accompanied by boycott power.

No one has shown this weapon to work so well as Don Wildmon of the American Family Association. His organization gets a large number of volunteers to monitor television programs for sex, violence, and anti-Christian bias.

When the greatest offenders are identified, sponsors are contacted and respectfully asked to withdraw their advertising from such programs. If there is no response or one of contempt for those with traditional values, Wildmon calls for a boycott of the products produced by corporations sponsoring such trash.

Effective? Consider this account in the *AFA Journal* of January, 1990:

"Mennen was the second leading sponsor of sex, violence and profanity during monitoring in 1988, tenth in 1987, second in 1986, and first in 1984. . . .

" . . . Mennen had to shut down for two weeks (over 350 employees laid off during that time) because truckloads of their products are being returned from stores and warehouses due to lack of sales. They are in financial trouble!"

Here is a crash program for those determined to use economic warfare to defend Christian freedom and prepare for crisis times:

1. Spend one-fourth of grocery-shopping budget on grains, beans (dried), and seeds for sprouting. The first two will provide a high-protein diet when store shelves are empty. Frank Ford, founder of Arrowhead Mills, told me years ago: "A grain and a bean is a whole protein, when eaten together." Sprouting seeds such as alfalfa and mung beans will give fresh food in your kitchen when no garden produce is available.

2. Buy "junk silver": i.e., coins through 1964 which have 90% silver content and will be real money to buy food and gas when paper money is worthless. Either get them from a reliable local coin dealer, or even a national dealer who is reliable like Franklin Sanders, (901) 373-3626.

3. Support only Christian works uncompromisingly Biblical. *Get out* of "churches" which deny the Virgin Birth of Christ, His Blood Atonement, or Resurrection. Study the Westminster Confession in Appendix H. Would God have you giving to works which depart from this Bible sum-

mary? Remember Matthew 6:19-21 and II Corinthians 6:14-18.

4. Since both Old and New Testaments teach that believers should tithe, or give ten percent to Almighty God, give that tithe and additional offerings strategically. A good mix is one-third to the local church; one-third to missions; one-third to Christian schools and colleges, or in support of home-schooling.

Strong resistance to these ideas may well indicate oppression from the powers of darkness.

Some need deliverance from demonic powers. If they repent, are truly broken, loving God and hating sin, this will not be difficult. My book, *Healing of the Mind,* tells how to go about spiritual warfare to set the captives free, in the name of Jesus Christ. All Christian families and leadership should be trained in these principles if they are to be effective in this day of increased satanism, witchcraft, New Age delusions, astrology, and the drug-induced sorcery which lies at the heart of substance abuse in our day.

What is needed is a college which trains young people in such principles, in the power of the Holy Spirit, by mature, godly instructors. The Bible must be applied in all academic disciplines and the skills necessary to rebuild lands in righteousness on top of the ruins and rubble of this present world system. Our present crisis comes because universities worldwide have been under the control of Marxist-Leninists and humanists who will not tolerate believers on the faculty or in administration.

A former dean of a state university told me he and the president of that university were both fired the same day and replaced with hardcore Reds who transformed the school into a communist training center within weeks. Why? They were Christian believers. Yet some naive souls still believe it is only in Red China or the USSR that such things take place. Indeed, the irony of our time is that multitudes despise communism who have lived under its heel for decades. Yet pampered, soft, undisciplined would-be intellectuals in the West still long for the viper's kiss.

Alexandr Solzhenitsyn, called a "prophet in exile" even by *Time* magazine reporter Paul Gray, had this to say at 70, after living in the United States for 14 years: "In Western Civilization — which used to be called Western-Christian but now might better be called Western-pagan — along with the development of intellectual life and science, there has been a loss of the serious moral basis of society. During these 300 years of Western Civilization, there has been a sweeping away of duties and expansion of rights. But we have two lungs. You can't breathe with just one lung and not with the other. We must avail ourselves of rights and duties in equal measure. And if this is not established by law, if the law does not oblige us to do that, then we have to control ourselves.

"When Western society was established, it was based on the idea that each individual limited his own behavior. Everyone understood what he could do and what he could not do. The law itself did not restrain people. Since then, the only things we have been developing are rights, rights, rights, at the expense of duty."[22]

Truth has a ring to it. Most people in the so-called "free" West who are not given over to the strong delusion of socialism's siren call know our permissive society has produced nothing but sin gone mad. Yet many insist that "democracy" is the opposing philosophy to Red totalitarianism. If that were so, why have the Soviets and other communists of our time insisted that their goal was "democratic socialism"?

No, Christianity is the only real alternative to socialism on this planet. In its Biblically revealed form, it is absolute truth. All other philosophies are lies, promoted by the one the Lord Jesus called "a murderer from the beginning...a liar, and the father of it."[23]

My book, *Return of the Puritans,* is subtitled "Christianity vs. Socialism in Mortal Combat." I have actually had to explain what that phrase means to some semi-literate products of American universities today! Many do not even know that in mortal combat, only one lives; the other dies. That book gives America's Christian history contrasted with the Kabalistic, Illuminati-spawned socialist takeover of our land.

No believer should ever fear this mortal combat. Anyone who has studied God's Word, especially the Book of Revelation, knows that all true followers of Jesus Christ are on the winning side. (That, by the way, is the reason New-Age witches and satanists are forbidden to read the Bible. A former witch told me they were being constantly told Lucifer would win the Battle of Armageddon and defeat Christ!)

We began this book stating that Almighty God is about to show who is King of Kings and Lord of Lords. And so we shall end it. The question is not *if* the Lord Jesus Christ is absolute victor, or *when* He will return, but that which the terrified Saul (who became Paul) asked Him on the road to Damascus after being blinded by His Glory: "Lord, what wilt thou have me to do?"[24]

Many Christians are receiving revelations of demonic darkness covering the land — not just America, but the whole world. One sister in Christ reported that she saw this darkness being pierced *only* where committed believers were consistent in fasting and prayer!

This report confirmed what God has been teaching me for years. Thus, I have been coordinating an effort, Deborah Fellowship, which the Lord laid on my heart years ago. (See Judges 4 and 5 for the way in which a woman who heard from God was used by Him to save her nation, in cooperation with his disciplined general, Barak, and a whole army from two of the tribes of Israel.) Although prayer and fasting are not specifically mentioned here, *praise*

112

for the results of them and action based on them surely are. Note that Deborah, unlike the squeamish, apathetic, and even cowardly folks you and I see daily, was able to "discern the signs of the times." In Judges 5:6-9 Deborah vividly describes a society such as ours: a fearful populace, where crime had emptied highways; extreme poverty where whole villages had lost their economic base, and therefore, their people; "new gods" or idolatry on such a scale that God said war was inevitable; total disarmament in the face of arrogant conquerors. Yet there were *willing* leaders and *willing* followers who volunteered to fight in the day of great crisis!

And so it is today. Yes, occultism and humanism, the "new gods," are rampant everywhere. Yes, our schools have been so radicalized by Marxist teachers that few young people have even seen the documents in the appendix of this book. (That is why they are there. *We must teach them the Christian heritage of America,* and pass on the *Mayflower Compact,* the *Declaration of Independence,* and the *Constitution* to the remnant people called to restore the Christian Republic they gave us.) Yes, there is an evil financial oligarchy which controls the money system, media, government and educational establishment of our day. *So what?*

Where is that faith that "laughs at impossibilities, and cries, it shall be done"? God is looking for fasting prayer warriors who can believe Him to slay giants, open iron doors, raise up praise-filled armies and take the kingdom for His glory!

Three times in Daniel, chapter 7, God says that the saints of the Most High shall take the kingdom and possess it forever! The context is one of great conflict and tribulation on the earth, where the Lord comes and ushers in the Judgment, as well as the saints' victory. Emphatically, Christian Reconstruction is not a fleshly effort to force a hostile world God's way! It is God's army moving, in total faith in Him and His Word, to do what He has told us to pray and do: "Thy kingdom come; Thy will be done in earth, as it is in heaven." Like the saints of all ages, we shall know victory "Not by might, nor by power, but by My Spirit, saith the LORD."[25]

My husband and I raised our children for God's glory, and He is working in and through them and their children for His glory. But what of those who never had such a heritage? What of those vast number of young and old, coming to Christ now, who have never been trained in His ways?

As I said earlier, a training center, even a college, is needed for the remnant leadership of the vast harvest of souls which God shall yet bring into His family to establish His kingdom "in earth, as it is in heaven."

As we get older, we can think of no greater priority to leave for the generations that are to come. To that end, we have established New Puritan Life, an affiliate under National Foundation of Annandale, Virginia, whose director is Dale Crowley. The Foundation provides a way for small works to receive tax-deductible gifts for worthy projects, and has approved the college endowment. A campus is now available here in the mountains for only two million dollars: 138 acres with 28 buildings, a summer camp facility, and two athletic fields! Deborah Fellowship is fasting and praying for a four-year college to be raised up there through New Puritan Life. Contributions will be made from the sale of this book to New Puritan Life toward this project. All authors of this work have agreed to accept no royalties, for we are all committed to this training center for leaders of God's remnant in the years to come. Our goal is for short-term sessions and seminars as soon as the campus is purchased; a four-year college by the year 2000. Donors who wish to contribute directly to the project should send their gifts to New Puritan Life, P.O. Box 1212, Fairview, NC 28730. Those wishing to have more details may phone me at New Puritan Library: (704) 628-2185. No part of the funds raised will be retained here at all. National Foundation takes a small percentage of the first $50,000 raised for administrative costs, after which the investment they make provides for that. Stewards of the Lord's money will realize that few missions or Christian organizations keep so little for administration.

For far too long we who believe in covenant theology, spiritual warfare, Biblical authority and inerrancy, and Constitutional government have been asked to support works which oppose one or more of these convictions. No more! Judgment has begun at the household of God. The fall of glitter-and-tinsel televangelism and cracks in the foundation of the Dispensational nightmare are part of that judgment. Now Almighty God is asking His people to wake up and grow up, not to swallow "cunningly devised fables" any longer, heaping up great quantities of "wood, hay and stubble" for burning. It is high time our tithes and offerings go where our *heart* is, so that our giving be as much "gold, silver and precious stones" as our fasting, praying, witnessing, evangelism, and Christian reconstruction are.

All-out war on error must be declared! We who are bond slaves of Jesus Christ must "earnestly contend for the faith once delivered to the saints."[26] Furthermore, we must fight for Christian freedom with every means at our disposal: in prayer and fasting, with time and talents, including all our financial resources.

One great wonder of the divine will is that total surrender to Jesus Christ sets the spirit free. In the words of Scripture, "If the Son therefore shall make you free, ye shall be free indeed."[27] In the words of ancient liturgy, "His service is perfect freedom."

Only those set free from the bondage of sin are fit to defend the Christian freedom needed to spread it worldwide.

America must become a Christian Republic again, or die. Let us hear no more of this propaganda about "democracy," where 50%-plus-one imagine they can outvote Almighty God! Study the cartoon contrast between a republic and a democracy by Rus Walton in Appendix E.

After Benjamin Franklin had, with 38 others, signed the U.S. Constitution on September 17, 1787, a woman ran up to him asking, "Sir, what kind of government do we have?"

"A republic, Madam, if you can keep it!" he answered.[28]

Some will sense the call to be a Deborah or Barak in God's army for fasting and prayer, piercing the darkness Satan has sent to destroy Christian freedom and our republic. If so, find at least one other to agree with you in prayer, and send NPL a postcard stating your intent, with your address and phone number. We shall count you in on Deborah Fellowship. If you can get the periodicals mentioned earlier in this chapter, look for direction for prayer from them. Very occasionally you may get a phone call with an urgent national or international prayer request, or even a state or local request, from a Deborah Fellowship coordinator.

Some good books for fellow intercessors were mentioned earlier. You may become an NPL "colporteur" (i.e., an individual who distributes Christian books and Bibles) to get them out to your prayer network, if you wish.

Other excellent books are the recent bestseller, *This Present Darkness,* by Frank Peretti, and *Claim Your Birthright,* by Jim McKeever. The former is a startling novel where a skeptical reporter and prayerful pastor discover a hideous New Age plot to subjugate their town and the whole human race. The latter is non-fiction: a powerful Scripture study of the fact that the church is Israel. It annihilates the Dispensational view that God has two chosen people, once and for all. McKeever quotes several pages from my book, *Hear, O Israel,* long out of print: the section that documents the non-Hebraic ancestry of the majority

116

of contemporary Jews. This information, of course, negates the Zionist-Dispensational claim of the Israelis to the Holy Land on the basis of Biblical prophecy.

All-important in the days of Great Conflict between light and darkness in the days ahead will be our outlook, our perspective. "Looking unto Jesus, the author and finisher of our faith," is the sure way to victory. Worry over Satan's plans — whether through the 1992 European Community or the Zionist financial oligarchy — is the sure path to defeat.

Like Nehemiah's "reconstructionists" of old, we must have a trowel in one hand and a weapon in the other, to see the victory. God has never needed a majority; only a remnant. Those willing to fight the spiritual warfare necessary to regain our freedom may well be the ones who rebuild in righteousness on top of the rubble of Satan's plans!

May we never be the spiritual "faulty salt" that would destroy America's godly remnant, just as physical faulty salt destroyed half of the Pilgrims that first awful winter in the Plymouth Colony. Let us hear and heed Founding Father and second President John Adams' prophetic warning:

"Posterity! You will never know what it cost the present generation to defend your freedoms. I hope you will make good use of it. If you do not, I shall repent in Heaven that I ever took half the pains to preserve it."[29]

FOOTNOTES

Chapter One

[1]Sobran, Joseph, "The Welfare State and Human Inaction," *National Review,* July 14, 1989, p. 46.

[2]*Mantooth Report,* July, 1989, Route 1, Box 387, Salem, IN 47167, p. 6.

[3]Courtney, Phoebe, *Audit the Fed.* TAX FAX #227, *The Independent American,* P.O. Box 636, Littleton, CO 80160 (75 cents), pp. 5-6.

[4]Plymouth Rock Foundation's FAC-Sheet #54, P.O. Box 577, Marlbrough, NH 03455, p.1.

[5]Tehan, William H., *Quarterly Comment* (8/89, P.R. Herzig and Co., 71 Broadway, New York, NY 10006, p. 2.

[6]*Strategic Investment,* 8/20/89, P.O. Box 2291, Washington, D.C. 20013.

[7]Ibid.

[8]*Myers' Finance and Energy,* Watershed Issue, 7/11/86, N. 7307 Division, Suite 204, Spokane, WA 99208, pp. 1-4.

[9]Tehan, Op. Cit., pp. 8-10.

[10]Revelation 18:10b and 11.

[11]Revelation 18:17, 18.

[12]*American Banker,* 7/31/75.

[13]*American Banker,* 7/24/89, p. 26.

[14]Czeschin, Robert W., *Pearl Harbor II,* Agora, Inc., 824 E. Baltimore, MD 21202, 1987, p. 14.

[15]Anderson, Jack, "Who Owns America?" *Parade,* 4/16/89, p. 4.

[16]Ibid., pp. 5, 6.

119

Chapter Two

[1]Kline, David, "Debt Write-Off Plan Would See California Become A Ward of Japan." *The National Educator,* P.O. Box 333, Fullerton, CA 92632 ($15 per year), Sept. 1989, p. 8.

[2]Ibid., p. 9.

[3]*The Moneychanger,* Box 341753, Memphis, TN 38184, December, 1987.

[4]Walt, Lewis, *The Eleventh Hour,* Caroline House Publishers, Inc., Ottawa, IL 1979, p. 34.

[5]Dean Chuck, *Nam Vet,* Point Man International, Box 440, Mountlake Terrace, WA 98043, 1988, p. 22.

[6]Ibid., p. 24.

[7]Ibid., pp. 25-26.

[8]Ibid., pp. 123, 124.

[9]Matthew 24:10-14.

[10]Loraine Boettner, *The Reformed Doctrine of Predestination,* Philadelphia: Presbyterian and Reformed Publishing Co., 1974, pp. 382, 383.

Chapter Three

[1]Brewer, Justice David J., *"United States: Christian Nation."* The Christian Committee, Box 481, Lakemore, OH 44250.

[2]McPherson, Dave, *Rapture?* New Puritan Library, 91 Lytle Road, Fletcher, NC 28732, 1987, p. 45.

[3]Coey, John Alan, *A Martyr Speaks,* New Puritan Library, 91 Lytle Road, Fletcher, NC 28732, 1988, pp. 2-3.

[4]Amos 3:3.

[5]II Chronicles 7:14.

Chapter Four

[1]*Christian News,* Box 168, New Haven, MO 63068, 12/23/85.

[2]*Christian News,* 10/21/85.

[3]Dale Crowley, *Christian! Not Judeo-Christian.* Reprint of radio program: *The King's Business,* P.O. Box 1, Washington DC 20044.

[4]*Christian News,* 10/23/87.

[5]*The Jewish Press,* 1/6/89, p. 49. Reprinted from *Kahane Speaks,* P.O. Box 425, Midwood Station, Brooklyn, NY 11230.

Chapter Six

[1]Their writings (and the writings and tapes of those listed above) are all available through Emissary Publications, 9205 SE Clackamas Road, Clackamas, OR 97015.

[2]See *The Secrets of the Federal Reserve*, by Eustace Mullins for full details.

[3]The overwhelming majority of the Jews presently living in the United States are Khazars. They are descendants of the Eastern European Jews imported by Jacob Schiff and Company around the turn of the century. They do *not* have Hebrew blood in their veins.

[4]A complete photographic reproduction of this article by Winston Churchill may be found in *Descent Into Slavery?* See pp. 74-76.

[5]See *The Law That Never Was*, by M. "Red" Beckman and Wm. Benson.

[6]For the fully documented facts behind this statement see *Descent Into Slavery?* by Des Griffin; *To Russia With Love — Major Racey Jordan's Diaries*, by Major Racey Jordan; *The Best Enemy Money Can Buy*, by Dr. Antony C. Sutton; and *Wall Street and the Bolshevik Revolution*, by Dr. Antony C. Sutton.

[7]For additional details, see *Six Pointed Star*, by Jewish author Dr. O. Graham, and *Fourth Reich of the Rich*, by Des Griffin, pp. 163-193.

Chapter Seven

[1]Job 1:9-11.

[2]Job 1:21b.

[3]Job 42:5.

[4]John 14:8 NASB.

[5]John 14:6: KJV-a: NASB-b.

[6]Daniel 11:32-33.

[7]Hebrews 12:4.

[8]John 15:20.

[9]John 16:1-3.

[10]Revelation 2:9-11.

[11]Revelation 3:9-13.

[12]Judges 5:23.

[13]Ezekiel 9:4-6.

[14]Hosea 4:6.

[15]Psalm 94:16.

[16]Ezekiel 22:30.

[17]Isaiah 59:15, 16a.

[18]Matthew 5:13.

[19]Elliot, Elisabeth, *Shadow of the Almighty,* New York: Harper & Row, 1958, p. 247.

[20]Matthew 22:14.

[21]Romans 11:29.

[22]*Time,* 7/24/89, p. 70.

[23]John 8:44.

[24]Acts 9:6.

[25]Zechariah 4:6b.

[26]Jude 3b.

[27]John 8:36.

[28]Pierce, Jan Payne, *The Patriot Primer,* New Puritan Library, 91 Lytle Road, Fletcher, NC 28732, 1987, p. 57.

[29]Ibid., p. 71.

The Mayflower Compact, 1620

"In the Name of God, Amen. We, whose names are underwritten, the Loyal Subjects of our dread Sovereign Lord King James, by the Grace of God, of Great Britain, France, and Ireland, King, Defender of the Faith, etc. Having undertaken for the Glory of God, and Advancement of the Christian Faith, and the Honour of our King and Country, a Voyage to plant the first Colony in the northern parts of Virginia; Do by these Presents, solemnly and mutually, in the Presence of God and one another, covenant and combine ourselves together into a civil Body Politick, for our better Ordering and Preservation, and Furtherance of the Ends aforesaid: And by Virtue hereof do enact, constitute, and frame, such just and equal Laws, Ordinances, Acts, Constitutions, and Officers, from time to time, as shall be thought most meet and convenient for the general Good of the Colony; unto which we promise all due Submission and Obedience. In Witness whereof we have hereunto subscribed our names at Cape-Cod the eleventh of November, in the Reign of our Sovereign Lord King James, of England, France, and Ireland, the eighteenth, and of Scotland, the fifty-fourth, Anno Domini 1620."

The Declaration of Independence

In Congress July 4, 1776

The Unanimous Declaration of the Thirteen United States of America

When in the course of human events, it becomes necessary for one people to dissolve the political bands which have connected them with another, and to assume among the powers of the earth, the separate and equal station to which the Laws of Nature and of *Nature's God* entitles them, a decent respect to the opinions of mankind requires that they should declare the causes which impel them to the separation.

We hold these truths to be self-evident, that all men are created equal, that they are endowed by their *Creator* with certain unalienable Rights, that among these are Life, Liberty and the pursuit of Happiness. That to secure these rights, Governments are instituted among Men, deriving their just powers from the consent of the governed. That whenever any Form of Government becomes destructive of these ends, it is the Right of the People to alter or to abolish it, and to institute new Government, laying its foundation on such principles and organizing its powers in such form, as to them shall seem most likely to effect their Safety and Happiness. *Prudence,* indeed, will dictate that Governments long established should not be changed for light and transient causes; and accordingly all experience hath shewn, that mankind are more disposed to suffer, while evils are sufferable, than to right themselves by abolishing the forms to which they are accustomed. But when a long train of abuses and usurpations, pursuing invariably the same Object, evinces a design to reduce them under absolute Despotism, it is their right, it is their duty, to throw off such Government, and to provide new Guards for their future security. Such has been the patient sufferance of these Colonies; and such is now the necessity which constrains them to alter their former Systems of Government. The history of the present King of Great Britain is a history of repeated injuries and usurpations, all having in direct object the establishment of an absolute Tyranny over these States. To prove this, let Facts be submitted to a candid world.

He has refused his Assent to Laws, the most wholesome and necessary for the public good.

He has forbidden his Governors to pass Laws of immediate and pressing importance, unless suspended in their operation till his Assent should be obtained; and when so suspended, he has utterly neglected to attend to them.

He has refused to pass other Laws for the accommodation of large districts of people, unless those people would relinquish the right of Representation in the Legislature, a right inestimable to them and formidable to tyrants only.

He has called together legislative bodies at places unusual, uncomfortable, and distant from the depository of their public Records, for the sole purpose of fatiguing them into compliance with his measures.

He has dissolved Representative Houses repeatedly, for opposing with manly firmness his invasions on the rights of the people.

He has refused for a long time, after such dissolutions, to

cause others to be elected; whereby the Legislative powers, incapable of Annihilation, have returned to the People at large for their exercise; the State remaining in the meantime exposed to all the dangers of invasion from without, and convulsions within.

He has endeavored to prevent the population of these States; for that purpose obstructing the Laws for Naturalization of Foreigners; refusing to pass others to encourage their migrations hither, and raising the conditions of new Appropriations of Lands.

He has obstructed the Administration of Justice, by refusing his Assent to Laws for establishing Judiciary Powers.

He has made Judges dependent on his Will alone, for the tenure of their offices, and the amount and payment of their salaries.

He has erected a multitude of New Offices, and sent hither swarms of Officers to harass our people, and eat out their substance.

He has kept among us, in times of peace, Standing Armies without the Consent of our legislature.

He has affected to render the Military independent of and superior to the Civil power.

He has combined with others to subject us to a jurisdiction foreign to our constitution, and unacknowledged by our loss giving his Assent to their Acts of pretended Legislation:

For quartering large bodies of armed troops among us:

For protecting them, by a mock Trial, from punishment for any Murders which they should commit on the Inhabitants of these States:

For cutting off our Trade with all parts of the world:

For imposing Taxes on us without our Consent:

For depriving us in many cases of the benefits of Trial by jury:

For transporting us beyond Seas to be tried for pretended

offences:

For abolishing the free System of English Laws in a neighboring Province, establishing therein an Arbitrary government, and enlarging its Boundaries so as to render it at once an example and fit instrument for introducing the same absolute rule into these Colonies:

For taking away our Charters, abolishing our most valuable Laws, and altering fundamentally the Forms of our Governments:

For suspending our own Legislatures, and declaring themselves invested with power to legislate for us in all cases whatsoever.

He has abdicated Government here, by declaring us out of his Protection and waging war against us.

He has plundered our seas, ravaged our Coasts, burnt our towns, and destroyed the lives of our people.

He is at this time transporting large Armies of foreign Mercenaries to complete the works of death, desolation and tyranny, already begun with circumstances of Cruelty and perfidy scarcely paralleled in the most barbarous ages, and totally unworthy the Head of a civilized nation.

He has constrained our fellow Citizens taken captive on the high Seas to bear Arms against their Country, to become the executioners of their friends and Brethren, or to fall themselves by their Hands.

He has excited domestic insurrections amongst us, and has endeavored to bring on the inhabitants of our frontiers, the merciless Indian Savages, whose known rule of warfare is an undistinguished destruction of all ages, sexes and conditions.

In every stage of these Oppressions We have Petitioned for Redress in the most humble terms. Our repeated Petitions have been answered only by repeated injury. A Prince, whose character is thus Marked by every act which may define a Tyrant, is unfit to be the ruler of a free people.

Nor have We been wanting in attentions to our British brethren. We have warned them from time to time of attempts by their legislature to extend an unwarrantable jurisdiction over us. We have reminded them of the circumstances of our emigration and settlement here. We have appealed to their native justice and magnanimity, and we have conjured them by the ties of our common kindred to disavow these usurpations, which would inevitably interrupt our connections and correspondence. They too have been deaf to the voice of justice and of consanguinity. We must therefore, acquiesce in the necessity which denounces our Separation, and hold them, as we hold the rest of mankind, Enemies in War, in Peace Friends.

WE, THEREFORE, the REPRESENTATIVES of the UNITED STATES OF AMERICA, IN GENERAL CONGRESS, Assembled, appealing to the *Supreme Judge of the world* for the rectitude of our intentions, do, in the Name, and by the authority of the good People of these Colonies, solemnly PUBLISH and DECLARE, That these United Colonies are, and of Right ought to be FREE AND INDEPENDENT States; that they are Absolved from all Allegiance to the British Crown, and that all political connection between them and the State of Great Britain, is and ought to be totally dissolved; and that as FREE AND INDEPENDENT STATES, they have full Power to levy War, conclude Peace, contract Alliances, establish Commerce, and to do all other Acts and Things which INDEPENDENT STATES may of right do. And for the support of this Declaration, with a firm reliance on the protection of *Divine Providence,* We mutually pledge to each other our Lives, our Fortunes, and our sacred Honor.

The Constitution of the United States of America

We the People of the United States, **in** Order to form a more perfect Union, establish Justice, insure domestic Tranquility, provide for the common defence, promote the general Welfare, and secure the Blessings of Liberty to ourselves and our Posterity, do ordain and establish this Constitution for the United States of America.

ARTICLE I.

SECTION 1. All legislative Powers herein granted shall be vested in a Congress of the United States, which shall consist of a Senate and House of Representatives.

SECTION 2. The House of Representatives shall be composed of Members chosen every second Year by the People of the several States, and the Electors in each State shall have the Qualifications requisite for Electors of the most numerous Branch of the State Legislature.

No Person shall be a Representative who shall not have attained to the Age of twenty-five Years, and been seven Years a Citizen of the United States, and who shall not, when elected, be an Inhabitant of that State in which he shall be chosen.

[Representatives and direct Taxes shall be apportioned among the several States which may be included within this Union,

[NOTE: This booklet presents the Constitution and all amendments in their original form. Items which have since been amended or superseded, as identified in the footnotes, are bracketed.]

according to their respective Numbers, which shall be determined by adding to the whole Number of free Persons, including those bound to Service for a Term of Years, and excluding Indians not taxed, three fifths of all other Persons.]* The actual Enumeration shall be made within three Years after the first Meeting of the Congress of the United States, and within every subsequent Term of ten Years, in such Manner as they shall by Law direct. The Number of Representatives shall not exceed one for every thirty Thousand,** but each State shall have at Least one Representative; and until such enumeration shall be made, the State of New Hampshire shall be entitled to chuse three, Massachusetts eight, Rhode-Island and Providence Plantations one, Connecticut five, New-York six, New Jersey four, Pennsylvania eight, Delaware one, Maryland six, Virginia ten, North Carolina five, South Carolina five, and Georgia three.

When vacancies happen in the Representation from any State, the Executive Authority thereof shall issue Writs of Election to fill such Vacancies.

The House of Representatives shall chuse their Speaker and other Officers; and shall have the sole Power of Impeachment.

Section 3. The Senate of the United States shall be composed of two Senators from each State, [chosen by the Legislature thereof,]*** for six Years; and each Senator shall have one Vote.

Immediately after they shall be assembled in Consequence of the first Election, they shall be divided as equally as may be into three Classes. The Seats of the Senators of the first Class shall be vacated at the Expiration of the second Year, of the second Class at the Expiration of the fourth Year, and of the third Class at the

---

*Changed by section 2 of the fourteenth amendment.

**Ratio in 1965 was one to over 410,000.

***Changed by section 1 of the seventeenth amendment.

Expiration of the sixth Year, so that one-third may be chosen every second Year; [and if Vacancies happen by Resignation, or otherwise, during the Recess of the Legislature of any State, the Executive thereof may make temporary Appointments until the next Meeting of the Legislature, which shall then fill such Vacancies.]*

No Person shall be a Senator who shall not have attained to the Age of thirty Years, and been nine Years a Citizen of the United States, and who shall not, when elected, be an Inhabitant of that State for which he shall be chosen.

The Vice President of the United States shall be President of the Senate, but shall have no Vote, unless they be equally divided.

The Senate shall chuse their other Officers, and also a President pro tempore, in the absence of the Vice President, or when he shall exercise the Office of President of the United States.

The Senate shall have the sole Power to try all Impeachments. When sitting for that Purpose, they shall be on Oath or Affirmation. When the President of the United States is tried, the Chief Justice shall preside: And no Person shall be convicted without the Concurrence of two thirds of the Members present.

Judgment in Cases of Impeachment shall not extend further than to removal from Office, and disqualification to hold and enjoy any Office of honor, Trust or Profit under the United States: but the Party convicted shall nevertheless be liable and subject to Indictment, Trial, Judgment and Punishment, according to Law.

SECTION 4. The Times, Places and Manner of holding Elections for Senators and Representatives, shall be prescribed in each State by the Legislature thereof; but the Congress may at any time by Law make or alter such Regulations, except as to the Place of Chusing Senators.

---

*Changed by clause 2 of the seventeenth amendment.

The Congress shall assemble at least once in every Year, and such Meeting shall [be on the first Monday in December,]** unless they shall by Law appoint a different Day.

Section 5. Each House shall be the Judge of the Elections, Returns and Qualifications of its own Members, and a Majority of each shall constitute a Quorum to do Business; but a smaller number may adjourn from day to day, and may be authorized to compel the Attendance of absent Members, in such Manner, and under such Penalties as each House may provide.

Each House may determine the Rules of its Proceedings, punish its Members for disorderly Behavior, and, with the Concurrence of two thirds, expel a Member.

Each House shall keep a Journal of its Proceedings, and from time to time publish the same, excepting such Parts as may in their Judgment require Secrecy; and the Yeas and Nays of the Members of either House on any question shall, at the Desire of one fifth of those Present, be entered on the Journal.

Neither House, during the Session of Congress, shall, without the Consent of the other, adjourn for more than three days, nor to any other Place than that in which the two Houses shall be sitting.

Section 6. The Senators and Representatives shall receive a Compensation for their Services, to be ascertained by Law, and paid out of the Treasury of the United States. They shall in all Cases, except Treason, Felony and Breach of the Peace, be privileged from Arrest during their Attendance at the Session of their respective Houses, and in going to and returning from the same; and for any Speech or Debate in either House, they shall not be questioned in any other Place.

No Senator or Representative shall, during the Time for which he was elected, be appointed to any civil Office under the Authority of the United States, which shall have been created, or the

---

**Changed by section 2 of the twentieth amendment.

Emoluments whereof shall have been encreased during such time; and no Person holding any Office under the United States, shall be a Member of either House during his Continuance in Office.

SECTION 7. All Bills for raising Revenue shall originate in the House of Representatives; but the Senate may propose or concur with Amendments as on other Bills.

Every Bill which shall have passed the House of Representatives and the Senate, shall, before it become a Law, be presented to the President of the United States; If he approve he shall sign it, but if not he shall return it, with his Objections to that House in which it shall have originated, who shall enter the Objections at large on their Journal, and proceed to reconsider it. If after such Reconsideration two thirds of that House shall agree to pass the Bill, it shall be sent, together with the Objections, to the other House, by which it shall likewise be reconsidered, and if approved by two thirds of that House, it shall become a Law. But in all such Cases the Votes of both Houses shall be determined by Yeas and Nays, and the Names of the Persons voting for and against the Bill shall be entered on the Journal of each House respectively. If any Bill shall not be returned by the President within ten Days (Sundays excepted) after it shall have been presented to him, the Same shall be a Law, in like Manner as if he had signed it, unless the Congress by their Adjournment prevent its Return, in which Case it shall not be a Law.

Every Order, Resolution, or Vote to which the Concurrence of the Senate and House of Representatives may be necessary (except on a question of Adjournment) shall be presented to the President of the United States; and before the Same shall take Effect, shall be approved by him, or being disapproved by him, shall be repassed by two thirds of the Senate and House of Representatives, according to the Rules and Limitations prescribed in the Case of a Bill.

SECTION 8. The Congress shall have Power To lay and collect Taxes, Duties, Imposts and Excises, to pay the Debts and provide for the common Defence and general Welfare of the United States; but all Duties, Imposts and Excises shall be uniform throughout the United States;

To borrow money on the credit of the United States;

To regulate Commerce with foreign Nations, and among the several States, and with the Indian Tribes;

To establish an uniform Rule of Naturalization, and uniform Laws on the subject of Bankruptcies throughout the United States;

To coin Money, regulate the Value thereof, and of foreign Coin, and fix the Standard of Weights and Measures;

To provide for the Punishment of counterfeiting the Securities and current Coin of the United States;

To establish Post Offices and post Roads;

To promote the Progress of Science and useful Arts, by securing for limited Times to Authors and Inventors the exclusive Right to their respective Writings and Discoveries;

To constitute Tribunals inferior to the supreme Court;

To define and punish Piracies and Felonies committed on the high Seas, and Offenses against the Law of Nations;

To declare War, grant Letters of Marque and Reprisal, and make Rules concerning Captures on Land and Water;

To raise and support Armies, but no Appropriation of Money to that Use shall be for a longer Term than two Years;

To provide and maintain a Navy;

To make Rules for the Government and Regulation of the land and naval Forces;

To provide for calling forth the Militia to execute the Laws of the Union, suppress Insurrections and repel Invasions;

To provide for organizing, arming, and disciplining the Militia, and for governing such Part of them as may be employed in the Service of the United States, reserving to the States respectively, the Appointment of the Officers, and the Authority of training the Militia according to the discipline prescribed by Congress;

To exercise exclusive Legislation in all Cases whatsoever, over such District (not exceeding teñ Miles square) as may, by Cession of particular States, and the acceptance of Congress, become the Seat of the Government of the United States, and to exercise like Authority over all Places purchased by the Consent of the Legislature of the State in which the Same shall be, for the Erection of Forts, Magazines, Arsenals, dock-Yards, and other needful Buildings;—And

To make all Laws which shall be necessary and proper for carrying into Execution the foregoing Powers, and all other Powers vested by this Constitution in the Government of the United States, or in any Department or Officer thereof.

SECTION 9. The Migration or Importation of such Persons as any of the States now existing shall think proper to admit, shall not be prohibited by the Congress prior to the Year one thousand eight hundred and eight, but a tax or duty may be imposed on such Importation, not exceeding ten dollars for each Person.

The privilege of the Writ of Habeas Corpus shall not be suspended, unless when in Cases of Rebellion or Invasion the public Safety may require it.

No Bill of Attainder or ex post facto Law shall be passed.

No capitation, or other direct, Tax shall be laid, unless in Proportion to the Census or Enumeration herein before directed to be taken.*

No Tax or Duty shall be laid on Articles exported from any State.

---

* But see the sixteenth amendment.

No Preference shall be given by any Regulation of Commerce or Revenue to the Ports of one State over those of another: nor shall Vessels bound to, or from, one State, be obliged to enter, clear, or pay Duties in another.

No Money shall be drawn from the Treasury, but in Consequence of Appropriations made by Law; and a regular Statement and Account of the Receipts and Expenditures of all public Money shall be published from time to time.

No Title of Nobility shall be granted by the United States: And no Person holding any Office of Profit or Trust under them, shall, without the Consent of the Congress, accept of any present, Emolument, Office, or Title, of any kind whatever, from any King, Prince, or foreign State.

SECTION 10. No State shall enter into any Treaty, Alliance, or Confederation; grant Letters of Marque and Reprisal; coin Money; emit Bills of Credit; make any Thing but gold and silver Coin a Tender in Payment of Debts; pass any Bill of Attainder, ex post facto Law, or Law impairing the Obligation of Contracts, or grant any Title of Nobility.

No State shall, without the Consent of the Congress, lay any Imposts or Duties on Imports or Exports, except what may be absolutely necessary for executing its inspection Laws: and the net Produce of all Duties and Imposts, laid by any State on Imports or Exports, shall be for the Use of the Treasury of the United States; and all such Laws shall be subject to the Revision and Controul of the Congress.

No State shall, without the Consent of Congress, lay any duty of Tonnage, keep Troops, or Ships of War in time of Peace, enter into any Agreement or Compact with another State, or with a foreign Power, or engage in War, unless actually invaded, or in such imminent Danger as will not admit of delay.

SECTION 1. The executive Power shall be vested in a **President** of the United States of America. He shall hold his Office **during** the Term of four Years, and, together with the Vice-President, chosen for the same Term, be elected, as follows.

Each State shall appoint, in such Manner as the Legislature thereof may direct, a Number of Electors, equal to the whole Number of Senators and Representatives to which the State may be entitled in the Congress: but no Senator or Representative, or Person holding an Office of Trust or Profit under the United States, shall be appointed an Elector.

[The Electors shall meet in their respective States, and vote by Ballot for two persons, of whom one at least shall not be an Inhabitant of the same State with themselves. And they shall make a List of all the Persons voted for, and of the Number of Votes for each; which List they shall sign and certify, and transmit sealed to the Seat of the Government of the United States, directed to the President of the Senate. The President of the Senate shall, in the Presence of the Senate and House of Representatives, open all the Certificates, and the Votes shall then be counted. The Person having the greatest Number of Votes shall be the President, if such Number be a Majority of the whole Number of Electors appointed; and if there be more than one who have such Majority, and have an equal Number of Votes, then the House of Representatives shall immediately chuse by Ballot one of them for President; and if no Person have a Majority, then from the five highest on the List the said House shall in like Manner chuse the President. But in chusing the President, the Votes shall be taken by States, the Representation from each State having one Vote; a quorum for this Purpose shall consist of a Member or Members from two thirds of the States, and a Majority of all the States shall be necessary to a Choice. In every Case, after the Choice of the **President,** the Person having the greatest Number of Votes of the Electors shall be the Vice President. But if there should remain two or more who have equal Votes, the Senate shall chuse from them by Ballot the Vice-President.]*

The Congress may determine the Time of chusing the Electors, and the Day on which they shall give their Votes; which Day shall be the same throughout the United States.

No person except a natural born Citizen, or a Citizen of the United States, at the time of the Adoption of this Constitution, shall be eligible to the Office of President; neither shall any Person be eligible to that Office who shall not have attained to the Age of thirty-five Years, and been fourteen Years a Resident within the United States.

**[In Case of the Removal of the President from Office, or of his Death, Resignation, or Inability to discharge the Powers and Duties of the said Office, the same shall devolve on the Vice President, and the Congress may by Law, provide for the Case of Removal, Death, Resignation or Inability, both of the President and Vice President, declaring what Officer shall then act as President, and such Officer shall act accordingly, until the Disability be removed, or a President shall be elected.]

The President shall, at stated Times, receive for his Services, a Compensation, which shall neither be encreased nor diminished during the Period for which he shall have been elected, and he shall not receive within that Period any other Emolument from the United States, or any of them.

Before he enter on the Execution of his Office, he shall take the following Oath or Affirmation:—"I do solemnly swear (or affirm) that I will faithfully execute the Office of President of the United

*Superseded by the twelfth amendment.
**This clause has been affected by the twenty-fifth amendment.

States, and will to the best of my Ability, preserve, protect and defend the Constitution of the United States."

SECTION 2. The President shall be Commander in Chief of the Army and Navy of the United States, and of the Militia of the several States, when called into the actual Service of the United States; he may require the Opinion in writing, of the principal Officer in each of the executive Departments, upon any subject relating to the Duties of their respective Offices, and he shall have Power to Grant Reprieves and Pardons for Offenses against the United States, except in Cases of Impeachment.

He shall have Power, by and with the Advice and Consent of the Senate, to make Treaties, provided two-thirds of the Senators present concur; and he shall nominate, and by and with the Advice and Consent of the Senate, shall appoint Ambassadors, other public Ministers and Consuls, Judges of the supreme Court, and all other Officers of the United States, whose Appointments are not herein otherwise provided for, and which shall be established by Law: but the Congress may by Law vest the Appointment of such inferior Officers, as they think proper, in the President alone, in the Courts of Law, or in the Heads of Departments.

The President shall have Power to fill up all Vacancies that may happen during the Recess of the Senate, by granting Commissions which shall expire at the End of their next Session.

SECTION 3. He shall from time to time give to the Congress Information of the State of the Union, and recommend to their Consideration such Measures as he shall judge necessary and expedient; he may, on extraordinary Occasions, convene both Houses, or either of them, and in Case of Disagreement between them, with Respect to the Time of Adjournment, he may adjourn them to such Time as he shall think proper; he shall receive Ambassadors and other public Ministers; he shall take Care that the Laws be faithfully executed, and shall Commission all the Officers of the United States.

SECTION 4. The President, Vice President and all civil Officers of the United States, shall be removed from Office on Impeachment for, and Conviction of, Treason, Bribery, or other high Crimes and Misdemeanors.

ARTICLE III.

SECTION 1. The judicial Power of the United States, shall be vested in one supreme Court, and in such inferior Courts as the Congress may from time to time ordain and establish. The Judges, both of the supreme and inferior Courts, shall hold their Offices during good Behaviour, and shall, at stated Times, receive for their Services, a Compensation, which shall not be diminished during their Continuance in Office.

SECTION 2. The judicial Power shall extend to all Cases, in Law and Equity, arising under this Constitution, the Laws of the United States, and Treaties made, or which shall be made, under their Authority;—to all Cases affecting Ambassadors, other public Ministers and Consuls;—to all Cases of admiralty and maritime Jurisdiction;—to Controversies to which the United States shall be a Party;—to Controversies between two or more States;— between a State and Citizens of another State;—between Citizens of different States;—between Citizens of the same State claiming Lands under Grants of different States, and between a State, or the Citizens thereof, and foreign States, Citizens or Subjects.

In all Cases affecting Ambassadors, other public Ministers and Consuls, and those in which a State shall be Party, the supreme Court shall have original Jurisdiction. In all the other Cases before mentioned, the supreme Court shall have appellate Jurisdiction, both as to Law and Fact, with such Exceptions, and under such Regulations as the Congress shall make.

The trial of all Crimes, except in Cases of Impeachment, shall be by Jury; and such Trial shall be held in the State where the said Crimes shall have been committed; but when not committed within any State, the Trial shall be at such Place or Places as the Congress may by Law have directed.

SECTION 3. Treason against the United States, shall consist only in levying War against them, or in adhering to their Enemies, giving them Aid and Comfort. No Person shall be convicted of Treason unless on the Testimony of two Witnesses to the same overt Act, or on Confession in open Court.

The Congress shall have Power to declare the Punishment of Treason, but no Attainder of Treason shall work Corruption of Blood, or Forfeiture except during the Life of the Person attainted.

ARTICLE IV.

SECTION 1. Full Faith and Credit shall be given in each State to the public Acts, Records, and judicial Proceedings of every other State. And the Congress may by general Laws prescribe the Manner in which such Acts, Records and Proceedings shall be proved, and the Effect thereof.

SECTION 2. The Citizens of each State shall be entitled to all Privileges and Immunities of Citizens in the several States.

A Person charged in any State with Treason, Felony, or other Crime, who shall flee from Justice, and be found in another State, shall on demand of the executive Authority of the State from which he fled, be delivered up, to be removed to the State having Jurisdiction of the Crime.

[No Person held to Service or Labour in one State, under the Laws thereof, escaping into another, shall, in Consequence of any Law or Regulation therein, be discharged from such Service or

Labour, but shall be delivered up on Claim of the Party to whom such Service or Labour may be due.]*

SECTION 3. New States may be admitted by the Congress into this Union; but no new State shall be formed or erected within the Jurisdiction of any other State; nor any State be formed by the Junction of two or more States, or parts of States, without the Consent of the Legislatures of the States concerned as well as of the Congress.

The Congress shall have Power to dispose of and make all needful Rules and Regulations respecting the Territory or other Property belonging to the United States; and nothing in this Constitution shall be so construed as to Prejudice any Claims of the United States, or of any particular State.

SECTION 4. The United States shall guarantee to every State in this Union a Republican Form of Government, and shall protect each of them against Invasion; and on Application of the Legislature, or of the Executive (when the Legislature cannot be convened) against domestic Violence.

ARTICLE V.

The Congress, whenever two-thirds of both Houses shall deem it necessary, shall propose Amendments to this Constitution, or, on the Application of the Legislatures of two-thirds of the several States, shall call a Convention for proposing Amendments, which, in either Case, shall be valid to all Intents and Purposes, as part of this Constitution, when ratified by the Legislatures of three-fourths of the several States, or by Conventions in three-fourths thereof, as the one or the other Mode of Ratification may be proposed by the Congress: Provided that no Amendment which may be made prior to the Year One thousand eight hundred and eight shall in any Manner affect the first and fourth Clauses in the

*Superseded by the thirteenth amendment.

Ninth Section of the first Article; and that no State, without its Consent, shall be deprived of its equal Suffrage in the Senate.

ARTICLE VI.

All Debts contracted and Engagements entered into, before the Adoption of this Constitution, shall be as valid against the United States under this Constitution, as under the Confederation.

This Constitution, and the Laws of the United States which shall be made in Pursuance thereof; and all Treaties made, or which shall be made, under the Authority of the United States, shall be the supreme Law of the Land; and the Judges in every State shall be bound thereby, any Thing in the Constitution or Laws of any State to the Contrary notwithstanding.

The Senators and Representatives before mentioned, and the Members of the several State Legislatures, and all executive and judicial Officers, both of the United States and of the several States, shall be bound by Oath or Affirmation, to support this Constitution; but no religious Test shall ever be required as a Qualification to any Office or public Trust under the United States.

ARTICLE VII.

The Ratification of the Conventions of nine States shall be sufficient for the Establishment of this Constitution between the States so ratifying the Same.

DONE in Convention by the Unanimous Consent of the States present the Seventeenth Day of September in the Year of our Lord one thousand seven hundred and Eighty seven and of the Independence of the United States of America the Twelfth.

In Witness whereof We have hereunto subscribed our Names.

Go *WASHINGTON*
Presidt and deputy from Virginia

New Hampshire.

John Langdon
Nicholas Gilman

Massachusetts.

Nathaniel Gorham
Rufus King

New Jersey.

Wil: Livingston
David Brearley.
Wm Paterson.
Jona: Dayton

Pennsylvania.

B Franklin
Robt. Morris
Thos. FitzSimons
James Wilson
Thomas Mifflin
Geo. Clymer
Jared Ingersoll
Gouv Morris

Delaware.

Geo: Read
John Dickinson
Jaco: Broom
Gunning Bedford jun
Richard Bassett

Connecticut.

Wm Saml Johnson
Roger Sherman

New York.

Alexander Hamilton

Maryland.

James McHenry
Danl Carrol
Dan: of St Thos Jenifer

Virginia.

John Blair
James Madison Jr.

North Carolina.

Wm Blount
Hu Williamson
Richd Dobbs Spaight.

South Carolina.

J. Rutledge
Charles Pinckney
Charles Cotesworth
  Pinckney
Pierce Butler

Georgia.

WILLIAM FEW
ABR BALDWIN

Attest:

WILLIAM JACKSON, *Secretary.*

ARTICLES IN ADDITION TO, AND AMENDMENT OF, THE CONSTITUTION OF THE UNITED STATES OF AMERICA, PROPOSED BY CONGRESS, AND RATIFIED BY THE LEGISLATURES OF THE SEVERAL STATES, PURSUANT TO THE FIFTH ARTICLE OF THE ORIGINAL CONSTITUTION.*

(The first 10 Amendments were ratified December 15, 1791, and form what is known as the "Bill of Rights")

AMENDMENT I

Congress shall make no law respecting an establishment of religion, or prohibiting the free exercise thereof; or abridging the freedom of speech, or of the press; or the right of the people peaceably to assemble, and to petition the Government for a redress of grievances.

AMENDMENT II

A well regulated Militia, being necessary to the security of a free State, the right of the people to keep and bear Arms, shall not be infringed.

AMENDMENT III

No Soldier shall, in time of peace be quartered in any house, without the consent of the Owner, nor in time of war, but in a manner to be prescribed by law.

---

*Amendment XXI was not ratified by state legislatures, but by state conventions summoned by Congress.

The right of the people to be secure in their persons, **houses,** papers, and effects, against unreasonable searches and **seizures,** shall not be violated, and no Warrants shall issue, but upon **proba-**ble cause, supported by Oath or affirmation, and particularly describing the place to be searched, and the persons or things to be seized.

AMENDMENT V

No person shall be held to answer for a capital, or otherwise infamous crime, unless on a presentment or indictment of a Grand Jury, except in cases arising in the land or naval forces, or in the Militia, when in actual service in time of War or public danger; nor shall any person be subject for the same offence to be twice put in jeopardy of life or limb; nor shall be compelled in any criminal case to be a witness against himself, nor be deprived of life, liberty, or property, without due process of law; nor shall private property be taken for public use, without just compensation.

AMENDMENT VI

In all criminal prosecutions, the accused shall enjoy the right to a speedy and public trial, by an impartial jury of the State and district wherein the crime shall have been committed, which dis-trict shall have been previously ascertained by law, and to be in-formed of the nature and cause of the accusation; to be confronted with the witnesses against him; to have compulsory process for obtaining witnesses in his favor, and to have the Assistance of Counsel for his defence.

AMENDMENT VII

In suits at common law, where the value in controversy shall exceed twenty dollars, the right of trial by jury shall be preserved, **and no** fact tried by a jury, shall be otherwise reexamined in **any**

Court of the United States, than according to the rules of the common law.

Excessive bail shall not be required, nor excessive fines imposed, nor cruel and unusual punishments inflicted.

AMENDMENT IX

The enumeration in the Constitution, of certain rights, shall not be construed to deny or disparage others retained by the people.

AMENDMENT X

The powers not delegated to the United States by the Constitution, nor prohibited by it to the States, are reserved to the States respectively, or to the people.

AMENDMENT XI

(Ratified February 7, 1795)

The Judicial power of the United States shall not be construed to extend to any suit in law or equity, commenced or prosecuted against one of the United States by Citizens of another State, or by Citizens or Subjects of any Foreign State.

AMENDMENT XII

(Ratified July 27, 1804)

The Electors shall meet in their respective states and vote by ballot for President and Vice-President, one of whom, at least, shall not be an inhabitant of the same state with themselves; they shall name in their ballots the person voted for as President, and in distinct ballots the person voted for as Vice-President, and they shall make distinct lists of all persons voted for as President, and of all persons voted for as Vice-President, and of the number of votes for each, which lists they shall sign and certify, and transmit sealed to the seat of the government of the United States, directed to the President of the Senate;—The President of the Senate shall, in presence of the Senate and House of Representatives, open all the certificates and the votes shall then be counted;— The person having the greatest number of votes for President, shall be the President, if such number be a majority of the whole number of Electors appointed; and if no person have such majority, then from the persons having the highest numbers not exceeding three on the list of those voted for as President, the House of Representatives shall choose immediately, by ballot, the President. But in choosing the President, the votes shall be taken by states, the representation from each state having one vote; a quorum for this purpose shall consist of a member or members from two-thirds of the states, and a majority of all the states shall be necessary to a choice. [And if the House of Representatives shall not choose a President whenever the right of choice shall devolve upon them, before the fourth day of March next following, then the Vice-President shall act as President, as in the case of the death or other constitutional disability of the President.—]* The person having the greatest number of votes as Vice-President, shall be the Vice-President, if such number be a majority of the whole number of Electors appointed, and if no person have a majority, then from the two highest numbers on the list, the Senate shall choose the Vice-President; a quorum for the purpose shall consist of two-thirds of the whole number of Senators, and a majority of the whole number shall be necessary to a choice. But no person constitutionally ineligible to the office of President shall be eligible to that of Vice-President of the United States.

*Superseded by section 3 of the twentieth amendment.

(Ratified December 6, 1865)

SECTION 1. Neither slavery nor involuntary servitude, except as a punishment for crime whereof the party shall have been duly convicted, shall exist within the United States, or any place subject to their jurisdiction.

SECTION 2. Congress shall have power to enforce this article by appropriate legislation.

AMENDMENT XIV

(Ratified July 9, 1868)

SECTION 1. All persons born or naturalized in the United States, and subject to the jurisdiction thereof, are citizens of the United States and of the State wherein they reside. No State shall make or enforce any law which shall abridge the privileges or immunities of citizens of the United States; nor shall any State deprive any person of life, liberty, or property, without due process of law; nor deny to any person within its jurisdiction the equal protection of the laws.

SECTION 2. Representatives shall be apportioned among the several States according to their respective numbers, counting the whole number of persons in each State, excluding Indians not taxed. But when the right to vote at any election for the choice of electors for President and Vice-President of the United States, Representatives in Congress, the Executive and Judicial officers of a State, or the members of the Legislature thereof, is denied to any of the male inhabitants of such State, being twenty-one years of age,* and citizens of the United States, or in any way abridged, except for participation in rebellion, or other crime, the basis of

*Changed by section 1 of the twenty-sixth amendment.

representation therein shall be reduced in the proportion which the number of such male citizens shall bear to the whole number of male citizens twenty-one years of age in such State.

SECTION 3. No person shall be a Senator or Representative in Congress, or elector of President and Vice-President, or hold any office, civil or military, under the United States, or under any State, who, having previously taken an oath, as a member of Congress, or as an officer of the United States, or as a member of any State legislature, or as an executive or judicial officer of any State, to support the Constitution of the United States, shall have engaged in insurrection or rebellion against the same, or given aid or comfort to the enemies thereof. But Congress may by a vote of two-thirds of each House, remove such disability.

SECTION 4. The validity of the public debt of the United States, authorized by law, including debts incurred for payment of pensions and bounties for services in suppressing insurrection or rebellion, shall not be questioned. But neither the United States nor any State shall assume or pay any debt or obligation incurred in aid of insurrection or rebellion against the United States, or any claim for the loss or emancipation of any slave; but all such debts, obligations and claims shall be held illegal and void.

SECTION 5. The Congress shall have power to enforce, by appropriate legislation, the provisions of this article.

AMENDMENT XV

(Ratified February 3, 1870)

SECTION 1. The right of citizens of the United States to vote shall not be denied or abridged by the United States or by any State on account of race, color, or previous condition of servitude—

SECTION 2. The Congress shall have power to enforce this article by appropriate legislation.

(Ratified February 3, 1913)

The Congress shall have power to lay and collect taxes on incomes, from whatever source derived, without apportionment among the several States, and without regard to any census or enumeration.

AMENDMENT XVII

(Ratified April 8, 1913)

The Senate of the United States shall be composed of two Senators from each State, elected by the people thereof, for six years; and each Senator shall have one vote. The electors in each State shall have the qualifications requisite for electors of the most numerous branch of the State legislatures.

When vacancies happen in the representation of any State in the Senate, the executive authority of such State shall issue writs of election to fill such vacancies: *Provided,* That the legislature of any State may empower the executive thereof to make temporary appointments until the people fill the vacancies by election as the legislature may direct.

This amendment shall not be so construed as to affect the election or term of any Senator chosen before it becomes valid as part of the Constitution.

AMENDMENT XVIII

(Ratified January 16, 1919)

[SECTION 1. After one year from the ratification of this article the manufacture, sale, or transportation of intoxicating liquors within, the importation thereof into, or the exportation thereof from the United States and all territory subject to the jurisdiction thereof for beverage purposes is hereby prohibited.

[SECTION 2. The Congress and the several States shall have concurrent power to enforce this article by appropriate legislation.

[SECTION 3. This article shall be inoperative unless it shall have been ratified as an amendment to the Constitution by the legislatures of the several States as provided in the Constitution, within seven years from the date of the submission hereof to the States by the Congress.]*

(Ratified August 18, 1920)

The right of citizens of the United States to vote shall not be denied or abridged by the United States or by any State on account of sex.

Congress shall have power to enforce this article by appropriate legislation.

(Ratified January 23, 1933)

SECTION 1. The terms of the President and Vice President shall end at noon on the 20th day of January, and the terms of Senators and Representatives at noon on the 3d day of January, of the years in which such terms would have ended if this article had not been ratified; and the terms of their successors shall then begin.

SECTION 2. The Congress shall assemble at least once in every year, and such meeting shall begin at noon on the 3d day of January, unless they shall by law appoint a different day.

SECTION 3. If, at the time fixed for the beginning of the term of the President, the President elect shall have died, the Vice President elect shall become President. If a President shall not have been chosen before the time fixed for the beginning of his term, or if the President elect shall have failed to qualify, then the Vice President elect shall act as President until a President shall have qualified; and the Congress may by law provide for the case

---

*Repealed by section 1 of the twenty-first amendment.

wherein neither a President elect nor a Vice President elect shall have qualified, declaring who shall then act as President, or the manner in which one who is to act shall be selected, and such person shall act accordingly until a President or Vice President shall have qualified.

SECTION 4. The Congress may by law provide for the case of the death of any of the persons from whom the House of Representatives may choose a President whenever the right of choice shall have devolved upon them, and for the case of the death of any of the persons from whom the Senate may choose a Vice President whenever the right of choice shall have devolved upon them.

SECTION 5. Sections 1 and 2 shall take effect on the 15th day of October following the ratification of this article.

SECTION 6. This article shall be inoperative unless it shall have been ratified as an amendment to the Constitution by the legislatures of three-fourths of the several States within seven years from the date of its submission.

AMENDMENT XXI

(*Ratified December 5, 1933*)

SECTION 1. The eighteenth article of amendment to the Constitution of the United States is hereby repealed.

SECTION 2. The transportation or importation into any State, Territory, or possession of the United States for delivery or use therein of intoxicating liquors, in violation of the laws thereof, is hereby prohibited.

SECTION 3. This article shall be inoperative unless it shall have been ratified as an amendment to the Constitution by conventions in the several States, as provided in the Constitution, within seven years from the date of the submission hereof to the States by the Congress.

(Ratified February 27, 1951)

SECTION 1. No person shall be elected to the office of the President more than twice, and no person who has held the office of President, or acted as President, for more than two years of a term to which some other person was elected President shall be elected to the office of the President more than once. But this Article shall not apply to any person holding the office of President when this Article was proposed by the Congress, and shall not prevent any person who may be holding the office of President, or acting as President, during the term within which this Article becomes operative from holding the office of President or acting as President during the remainder of such term.

SECTION 2. This article shall be inoperative unless it shall have been ratified as an amendment to the Constitution by the legislatures of three-fourths of the several States within seven years from the date of its submission to the States by the Congress.

AMENDMENT XXIII

(Ratified March 29, 1961)

SECTION 1. The District constituting the seat of Government of the United States shall appoint in such manner as the Congress may direct:

A number of electors of President and Vice President equal to the whole number of Senators and Representatives in Congress to which the District would be entitled if it were a State, but in no event more than the least populous State; they shall be in addition to those appointed by the States, but they shall be considered, for the purposes of the election of President and Vice President, to be electors appointed by a State; and they shall meet in the District and perform such duties as provided by the twelfth article of amendment.

Section 2. The Congress shall have power to enforce this article by appropriate legislation.

AMENDMENT XXIV

(Ratified January 23, 1964)

Section 1. The right of citizens of the United States to vote in any primary or other election for President or Vice President, for electors for President or Vice President, or for Senator or Representative in Congress, shall not be denied or abridged by the United States or any State by reason of failure to pay any poll tax or other tax.

Section 2. The Congress shall have power to enforce this article by appropriate legislation.

AMENDMENT XXV

(Ratified February 10, 1967)

Section 1. In case of the removal of the President from office or of his death or resignation, the Vice President shall become President.

Section 2. Whenever there is a vacancy in the office of the Vice President, the President shall nominate a Vice President who shall take office upon confirmation by a majority vote of both Houses of Congress.

Section 3. Whenever the President transmits to the President pro tempore of the Senate and the Speaker of the House of Representatives his written declaration that he is unable to discharge the powers and duties of his office, and until he transmits to them a written declaration to the contrary, such powers and duties shall be discharged by the Vice President as Acting President.

Section 4. Whenever the Vice President and a majority of either the principal officers of the executive departments or of such other body as Congress may by law provide, transmit to the

President pro tempore of the Senate and the Speaker of the House of Representatives their written declaration that the President is unable to discharge the powers and duties of his office, the Vice President shall immediately assume the powers and duties of the office as Acting President.

Thereafter, when the President transmits to the President pro tempore of the Senate and the Speaker of the House of Representatives his written declaration that no inability exists, he shall resume the powers and duties of his office unless the Vice President and a majority of either the principal officers of the executive department or of such other body as Congress may by law provide, transmit within four days to the President pro tempore of the Senate and the Speaker of the House of Representatives their written declaration that the President is unable to discharge the powers and duties of his office. Thereupon Congress shall decide the issue, assembling within forty-eight hours for that purpose if not in session. If the Congress, within twenty-one days after receipt of the latter written declaration, or, if Congress is not in session, within twenty-one days after Congress is required to assemble, determines by two-thirds vote of both Houses that the President is unable to discharge the powers and duties of his office, the Vice President shall continue to discharge the same as Acting President; otherwise, the President shall resume the powers and duties of his office.

AMENDMENT XXVI

(Ratified July 1, 1971)

SECTION 1. The right of citizens of the United States, who are eighteen years of age or older, to vote shall not be denied or abridged by the United States or by any State on account of age.

SECTION 2. The Congress shall have power to enforce this article by appropriate legislation.

50 EVIDENCES
THAT THE U.S.A. IS
"CONSTITUTIONALLY CHRISTIAN"!

The United States of America has a deeply-rooted spiritual heritage. In addition to the nation's united expression of faith in God, each individual state has separately acknowledged God as Sovereign and as the Author of liberty. The Legislative Service of the Library of Congress has compiled the provisions of State constitutions relative to the Supreme Being.

☆☆☆☆☆☆☆☆☆☆☆☆☆☆☆☆☆☆☆☆☆☆

ALABAMA (Constitution of 1901, 1963 supp.)

We, the people of the State of Alabama, in order to establish justice, . . . , invoking the favor and guidance of *Almighty God*, do ordain and establish. . . . *Preamble to Constitution*

. . . that they (all men) are endowed by their *Creator* with certain inalienable rights . . . Art. I, sec. 1 (Declaration of Rights).

ALASKA (Constitution of 1956, 1963 supp.)

We the people of Alaska, grateful to *God* . . . establish this Constitution. . . . *Preamble to Constitution*

ARIZONA (Constitution of 1910, 1963 supp.)

We, the people of the State of Arizona, grateful to *Almighty God* for our liberties, do ordain this Constitution. *Preamble to Constitution.*

ARKANSAS (Constitution of 1874, 1963 supp.)

We, the people of the State of Arkansas, grateful to *Almighty God* (establish this Constitution) . . . *Preamble to Constitution.*

All men have a natural and indefeasible right to worship *Almighty God* according to the dictates of their own consciences. . . . Art. 2, sec. 24.

No person who denies the *being of a God* shall hold any office in the civil departments of this State, nor be competent to testify as a witness in any court. Art. 19, sec. 1.

Religion, morality and knowledge being essential to good government, the General Assembly shall enact suitable laws to protect every religious denomination in the peaceable enjoyment of its own mode of public worship. Art. 2, sec. 25.

CALIFORNIA (Constitution of 1879, 1963 supp.)

We, the People of the State of California, grateful to Almighty God for our freedom, (establish this Constitution) . . . *Preamble to Constitution.*

COLORADO (Constitution of 1876, 1961 supp.)

We, the people of Colorado, with profound reverence for the *Supreme Ruler of the Universe* (establish this Constitution) . . . *Preamble to Constitution.*

CONNECTICUT (Constitution, 1963 supp.)

The People of Connecticut acknowledging with gratitude, the good providence of *God*, in having permitted them to enjoy a free government. . . . (establish this Constitution) *Preamble to Constitution.*

It being the duty of all men to worship the *Supreme Being,* the *Great Creator and Preserver of the Universe,* and their right to render that worship, in the mode most consistent with the dictates of their consciences (certain rights will follow; for full text see below) . . . Article Seventh, sec. 1.

DELAWARE (Constitution of 1897, 1962 supp.)

Through Divine goodness, all men have by nature the rights of worshiping and serving their *Creator* according to the dictates of their consciences. . . . *Preamble to Constitution.*

Although it is the duty of all men frequently to assemble together for the public worship of *Almighty God;* and piety and morality, on which the prosperity of communities depends, are hereby promoted; yet no man shall or ought to be compelled to attend any religious worship, to contribute to the erection or support of any place of worship, or to the maintenance of any ministry, against his own free will and consent; and no power shall or ought to be vested in or assumed by any magistrate that shall in any case interfere with, or in any manner control the rights of conscience, in the free exercise of religious worship, nor a preference given by law to any religious societies, denominations, or modes of worship. Art. I, sec. 1.

FLORIDA (Constitution of 1885, 1963 supp.)

We, the people of the State of Florida, grateful to *Almighty God* for our constitutional liberty . . . (establish this Constitution) *Preamble to Constitution.*

GEORGIA (Constitution of 1945, 1963 supp.)

All men have the natural and inalienable right to worship *God*, each according to the dictates of his own conscience. . . . Art. 1, sec. 2-112.

. . . we, the people of Georgia, relying upon the protection and guidance of *Almighty God*, do ordain and establish this Constitution. *Preamble to Constitution.*

HAWAII (Constitution, 1961 supp.)

We, the people of the State of Hawaii, grateful for *Divine Guidance* . . . (establish this constitution). *Preamble to Constitution.*

IDAHO (Constitution of 1890, 1961 supp.)

We, the people of the state of Idaho, grateful to *Almighty God* for our freedom. . . . (establish this Constitution). *Preamble to Constitution.*

It is ordained by the state of Idaho that perfect toleration of religious sentiment shall be secured, and no inhabitant of said state shall ever be molested in person or property on account of his or her mode of religious worship. . . . Art. 21, sec. 19.

ILLINOIS (Constitution of 1870, 1962 supp.)

We, the people of the State of Illinois — grateful to *Almighty God* for the civil, political and religious liberty which He hath so long permitted us to enjoy, and looking to Him for a blessing upon our endeavors to secure and transmit the same unimpaired to succeeding generations . . . (establish this Constitution) *Preamble to Constitution.*

160

INDIANA (Constitution of 1851, 1963 supp.)

We, the People of the State of Indiana, grateful to *Almighty God* for the free exercise of the right to choose our form of government, do ordain this Constitution. *Preamble to Constitution.*

We declare, That all men are created equal; that they are endowed by their *Creator* with certain unalienable rights . . ." Art, 1, sec. 1.

All men shall be secured in their natural right to worship *Almighty God* . . ." Art. 1, sec. 2.

IOWA (Constitution of 1857, 1963 supp.)

We, the People of the State of Iowa, grateful to the *Supreme Being* for the blessings hitherto enjoyed, and feeling our dependence on Him for a continuation of these blessings . . . (establish this Constitution) *Preamble to Constitution.*

KANSAS (Constitution of 1859, 1963 supp.)

We, the People of Kansas, grateful to *Almighty God* for our civil and religious privileges . . . (establish this constitution). *Preamble to Constitution.*

The right to worship God according to the dictates of conscience shall never be infringed. . . . *Bill of Rights,* sec. 7.

KENTUCKY (Constitution of 1956, 1962 supp.)

We, the people of the Commonwealth of Kentucky, grateful to *Almighty God* for the civil, political and religious liberties we enjoy . . . (establish this Constitution). *Preamble to Constitution.*

The right of worshiping *Almighty God* according to the dictates of their consciences. *Bill of Rights,* sec. 1.

LOUISIANA (Constitution of 1921, 1963 supp.)

Every person has the natural right to worship *God* according to the dictates of his own conscience. . . . Art. 1, sec. 4.

We, the people of the State of Louisiana, grateful to *Almighty God* for the civil, political and religious liberties we enjoy, and desiring to secure the continuance of these blessings, do ordain and establish this Constitution. *Preamble to Constitution.*

MAINE (Constitution, 1963 supp.)

We the people of Maine . . . acknowledging with grateful hearts the goodness of the *Sovereign Ruler of the Universe* in affording us an opportunity, so favorable to the design; and, imploring His aid and direction . . . (establish this Constitution). *Preamble to Constitution.*

All men have a natural and unalienable right to worship *Almighty God* according to the dictates of their own consciences. . . . Art. I, sec. 3.

MARYLAND (Constitution of 1867, 1963 supp.)

We, the people of the State of Maryland, grateful to *Almighty God* for our civil and religious liberty (declare specified rights) . . . *Preamble to Declaration of Rights.*

That as it is the duty of every man to worship *God* in such manner as he thinks most acceptable to Him, all persons are equally entitled to protection in their religious liberty. . . . Art. 36.

MASSACHUSETTS (Constitution of 1780, 1962 supp.)

We, therefore, the people of Massachusetts, acknowledging, with grateful hearts, the goodness of the *great Legislator of the universe,* in affording us, in the course of His providence, (an opportunity to form a compact); . . . and devoutly imploring His direction in so interesting a design, . . . (establish the Constitution). *Preamble to Constitution.*

It is the right as well as the duty of

all men in society, publicly, and at stated seasons to worship the *Supreme Being*, the *great Creator and Preserver of the universe*. . . . *Declaration of Rights*, Art. II.

As the public worship of *God* and instructions in piety, religion and morality, promote the happiness and prosperity of a people and the security of republican government (certain rights accrue to religious societies). *Declaration of Rights*, Art. III.

MICHIGAN (Constitution of 1908, 1963 supp.)

We, the people of the State of Michigan, grateful to *Almighty God* for the blessings of freedom . . . (establish the Constitution). *Preamble to Constitution*.

Every person shall be at liberty to worship *God* according to the dictates of his own conscience. . . . Art. II, sec. 3.

Religion, morality and knowledge being necessary to good government and the happiness of mankind, schools and the means of education shall forever be encouraged. Art. XI, sec. 1.

MONTANA (Constitution of 1889, 1961 supp.)

We, the people of Montana, grateful to *Almighty God* for the blessings of liberty (establish this Constitution). . . . *Preamble to Constitution*.

MINNESOTA (Constitution of 1857, 1963 supp.)

We, the people of the State of Minnesota, grateful to *God* for our civil and religious liberty, and desiring to perpetuate its blessings . . . (establish the Constitution). *Preamble to Constitution*.

The right of every man to worship God according to the dictates of his own conscience shall never be infringed. . . . Bill of Rights, Art. I, sec. 16.

MISSISSIPPI (Constitution of 1890, 1962 supp.)

We, the people of Mississippi in convention assembled, grateful to Almighty God, and invoking His blessing on our work, do ordain and establish this constitution. *Preamble to Constitution*.

No person who denies the existence of a *Supreme Being* shall hold any office in this state. Art. 14, sec. 265.

MISSOURI (Constitution of 1945, 1963 supp.)

We, the people of Missouri, with profound reverence for the *Supreme Ruler* of the Universe, and grateful for His goodness . . . (establish this Constitution). *Preamble to Constitution*.

That all men have a natural and indefeasible right to worship *Almighty God* according to the dictates of their own consciences . . . *Bill of Rights*, Art. I, sec. 5.

NEBRASKA (Constitution of 1876, 1963 supp.)

We, the people, grateful to Almighty God for our freedom, . . . (establish this Constitution). *Preamble to Constitution*.

All persons have a natural and indefeasible right to worship *Almighty God* according to the dictates of their own consciences. . . . *Bill of Rights*, Art. I, sec. 4.

NEVADA (Constitution of 1864, 1963 supp.)

We the people of the State of Nevada grateful to *Almighty God* for our freedom . . . (establish this Constitution). *Preamble to Constitution*.

NEW HAMPSHIRE (Constitution of 1783, 1963 supp.)

As morality and piety, rightly grounded on evangelical principles, will give the best and greatest security to government, and will lay, in the hearts of men, the strongest obligations to due subjection; and as the knowledge of these is most likely to be propagated through a society, by the institution of the public worship of the *Deity,* and of public instruction in morality and religion; therefrom, to promote these important purposes, the people of this state have a right to empower, and do hereby fully empower, the legislature, to authorize, from time to time, the several towns, parishes, bodies corporate, or religious societies, within this state, to make adequate provision, at their own expense, for support and maintenance of public Protestant teachers of piety, religion, and morality. . . .

And every denomination of Christians, demeaning themselves quietly, and as good subjects of the state, shall be equally under the protection of the law: And no subordination of any one sect or denomination to another, shall ever be established by law. . . . Pt. I, Art. 6th.

NEW JERSEY (Constitution of 1947, 1963 supp.)

We, the people of the State of New Jersey, grateful to *Almighty God* for the civil and religious liberty which He hath so long permitted us to enjoy, and looking to Him for a blessing upon our endeavors . . . (establish this Constitution). *Preamble to Constitution.*

No person shall be deprived of the inestimable privilege of worshipping *Almighty God* in a manner agreeable to the dictates of his own conscience. . . . Art. I, sec. 3.

NEW MEXICO (Constitution of 1911, 1959 supp.)

We, the people of New Mexico, grateful to *Almighty God* for the blessings of liberty . . . (Establish this Constitution). *Preamble to Constitution.*

Every man shall be free to worship *God* according to the dictates of his own conscience. . . . Art. II, sec. 11.

NEW YORK (Constitution of 1938, 1963 supp.)

We, the people of the State of New York, grateful to *Almighty God* for our Freedom, in order to secure its blessings, do establish this Constitution. *Preamble to Constitution.*

NORTH CAROLINA (Constitution of 1868, 1963 supp.)

We, the people of the State of North Carolina, grateful to *Almighty God,* the Sovereign Ruler of nations, for the preservation of the American Union and the existence of our civil, political and religious liberties, and acknowledging our dependence upon Him for the continuance of those blessings to us . . . (establish this Constitution). *Preamble to Constitution.*

All persons have a natural and inalienable right to worship *Almighty God* according to the dictates of their own consciences. . . . Art. 1, sec. 26.

The following classes of persons shall be disqualified for office: First, all persons who shall deny the *being of Almighty God* . . . Art. VI, sec. 8.

NORTH DAKOTA (Constitution of 1889, 1960 supp.)

We, the people of North Dakota, grateful to *Almighty God* for the blessings of civil and religious liberty, do ordain and establish this constitution.

OHIO (Constitution of 1851, 1963 supp.)

We, the people of the State of Ohio, grateful to *Almighty God* for our freedom, . . . (establish this Constitution). *Preamble to Constitution.*

. . . Religion, morality, and knowledge, however, being essential to good government, it shall be the duty of the general assembly to pass suitable laws to protect every religious denomination in the peaceable enjoyment of its own mode of public worship, and to encourage schools and the means of instruction. *Bill of Rights.* Art. I, sec. 7

OKLAHOMA (Constitution of 1907, 1963 supp.)

Invoking the guidance of *Almighty God*, in order to secure and perpetuate the blessing of liberty (we establish this Constitution) . . . *Preamble to Constitution.*

. . . Perfect toleration of religious sentiment shall be secured, and no inhabitant of the State shall ever be molested in person or property on account of his or her mode of religious worship; and no religious test shall be required for the exercise of civil or political rights. . . . Art. I, sec. 2.

OREGON (Constitution of 1859, 1961 supp.)

All men shall be secure in the Natural right, to worship *Almighty God* according to the dictates of their consciences. *Bill of Rights,* Art. I, sec. 2.

No law shall in any case whatever control the free exercise, and enjoyment of religious opinions, or interfere with the rights of conscience. *Bill of Rights,* Art. I, sec. 3.

PENNSYLVANIA (Constitution of 1874, 1963 supp.)

We, the people of . . . Pennsylvania, grateful to *Almighty God* for the blessings of civil and religious liberty, and humbly invoking His guidance, do ordain and establish this Constitution. *Preamble to Constitution.*

All men have a natural and indefeasible right to worship *Almighty God* according to the dictates of their own consciences. . . . Art. I, sec. 3.

. . . No person who acknowledges the being of a God and a future state of rewards and punishment shall, on account of his religious sentiments, be disqualified to hold any office or place of trust or profit under this Commonwealth. Art. I, sec. 4.

RHODE ISLAND (Constitution, 1963 supp.)

We, the people of the state of Rhode Island . . . , grateful to *Almighty God* for the civil and religious liberty which He hath so long permitted us to enjoy, and looking to Him for a blessing upon our endeavors to secure and transmit the same . . . (establish this Constitution). *Preamble to Constitution.*

. . . Whereas *Almighty God* hath created the mind free; and all attempts to influence it by temporal punishments or burdens, or by civil incapacitations, tend to beget habits of hypocrisy and meanness; and whereas a principal object of our venerable ancestors, in their migration to this country and their settlement of this state, was, as they expressed it, to hold forth a lively experiment, that a flourishing civil state may stand and be best maintained with full liberty in religious concernments: we, therefore, declare that no man shall be compelled to frequent or to support any religious worship, place, or ministry whatever, except in fulfillment of his own voluntary contract; nor enforced, restrained, molested, or burdened in his body or goods; nor disqualified from holding any office; nor otherwise suffer on account of his religious belief; and that every man shall be free to worship *God* according to the dictates of his own conscience, and to profess and by argument to maintain his opinion in matters of religion; and that the same shall in no wise diminish, enlarge, or affect his civil capacity. Art. I, sec. 3.

SOUTH CAROLINA (Constitution of 1895, 1963 supp.)

No person who denies the existence of a *Supreme Being* shall hold any office under this Constitution. Art. 17, sec. 4.

We, the people of the State of South Carolina, . . . grateful to *God* for our liberties, do ordain and establish this Constitution for the preservation and perpetuation of the same. *Preamble to Constitution.*

SOUTH DAKOTA (Constitution, 1961 supp.)

We, the people of South Dakota, grateful to *Almighty God* for our civil and religious liberties . . . (establish this Constitution). *Preamble to Constitution.*

The right to worship *God* according to the dictates of conscience shall never be infringed. . . . Art. VI, sec. 3.

TENNESSEE (Constitution of 1870, 1963 supp.)

That all men have a natural and indefeasible right to worship *Almighty God* according to the dictates of their own conscience. . . . Art. I, sec. 3.

No person who denies the *being of God*, or a future state of rewards and punishments, shall hold any office in the civil department of this State. Art. IX, sec. 2.

TEXAS (Constitution of 1876, 1963 supp.)

Humbly invoking the blessings of *Almighty God* . . . (we establish this Constitution). *Preamble to Constitution.*

. . . Nor shall any one be excluded from holding office on account of his religious sentiments, provided he acknowledge the existence of a *Supreme Being.* Art. I, sec. 4.

UTAH (Constitution, 1961 supp.)

Grateful to *Almighty God* for life and liberty, we . . . establish this Constitution. *Preamble to Constitution.*

VERMONT (Constitution of 1793, 1963 supp.)

That all men have a natural and unalienable right, to worship *Almighty God,* according to the dictates of their own consciences . . . every sect or denomination of Christians ought to observe the sabbath or Lord's day, and keep up some sort of religious worship, which to them shall seem more

agreeable to the revealed will of *God.* Ch. I, art. 3rd.

VIRGINIA (Constitution of 1902, 1962 supp.)

That religion or the duty which we owe to our *Creator* . . . can be directed only by reason and conviction, not by force or violence . . . (for full text, see below. Art. I, sec. 16.

WASHINGTON (Constitution of 1889, 1961 supp.)

We, the people of the State of Washington, grateful to the *Supreme Ruler of the Universe* for our liberties, do ordain this constitution. *Preamble to Constitution.*

WEST VIRGINIA (Constitution of 1872, 1963 supp.)

No man shall be compelled to frequent or support any religious worship . . . whatsoever; nor shall any man be enforced, restrained, molested or burthened, in his body or goods, or otherwise suffer, on account of his religious opinions or belief, but all men shall be free to profess, and by argument, to maintain their opinions in matters of religion; . . III, sec. 15.

WISCONSIN (Constitution of 1848, 1963 supp.)

We, the people of Wisconsin, grateful to *Almighty God* for our freedom . . . (establish this Constitution). *Preamble to Constitution.*

The right of every man to worship *Almighty God* according to the dictates of his own conscience shall never be infringed. . . . Art. I, sec. 18.

WYOMING (Constitution of 1890, 1963 supp.)

We, the people of the State of Wyoming, grateful to *God* for our civil, political and religious liberties . . . (establish this constitution). *Preamble to Constitution.*   ☆☆☆

Being a brief consideration
of the distinctions between
the great Biblical principles
on which the
American constitutional republic
was founded
and the malignant doctrines
of "democracy"
into which this nation has fallen.

(Reprinted by permission of the Plymouth Rock Foundation, P.O. Box 425, Marlborough, NH 03455.)

167

REPUBLIC

DEMOCRACY

GOVERNMENT BASED ON GOD'S LAW

Bible is textbook of govt. Law based on God's law. Constitution guarantees individual freedom, defines proper functions of govt. Minority rights upheld. (Ex 20:1-17, 24:3; Dt 4:1-9, 17:18-19; Isa 33:22; Gal 5:1.)

MAN'S GOVERNMENT (Humanism)

State is "god," "vox populi" is sovereign. Majority rule, minority rights suppressed. God's law denied, humanism is state "religion." (1 Sam 8:7; 2 Chron 7:19-22, Isa 1:21-26; Mk 7:20-23; Rom 1: 21-25, 8:7.)

REPRESENTATIVE GOVERNMENT

Power flows from God to citizen to representatives. People elect legislators, executives, judges. Officials accountable to electorate. Rights & due process upheld. (Ex 18:19-25, 19:5-8; Lev 19:15; Dt 1:13-18, 16:18-20; Rom 13:1-6; Tim 3:1-13.)

DIRECT GOVERNMENT (Mobocracy)

The people rule by emotion, legislate on impulse, judge by vote. No absolutes. Reason replace righteousness, majority decrees "justice." (Gen 11:1-9; Ex 23:1-2; Judges 21:25; Isa 59:1-15.)

LIMITED GOVERNMENT

God is Sovereign, govt. His minister of justice. Citizens restrict govt. power, divide it between fed, state & local levels, erect checks & balances. (Num 16:1-3; Dt 10:12-14, 11:1; Josh 22:14; Ps 22:28; Acts 5:29, 17:7; Rom 13:3-4; 1 Tim 6:15.)

CENTRALIZED GOVERNMENT (Tyranny)

Federal govt. unrestrained, local govts. mere appendages. Controls and bureaucracies sap nation's resources. Caesar is arbiter of morals, "truth" is what serves State (1 Sam 8:14-18; Isa 3:1-15; John 19:15.)

168

REPUBLIC   DEMOCRACY

PROPERTY RIGHTS SECURE

All property is God's, entrusted to individuals as His vice regents. Man has property in self, in rights & estate. Govt's function is to protect person and property (Ex 20:15-17, 22:3, 30:15; Lev 27:30-33; Num 5:6-8; Ps 24:1; 1 Cor 10:26.)

TAXATION (Confiscation)

Taxation an instrument of social control, citizens made servants of State. Personal property progressively taxed to support Caesar's excesses. (Lev 19:13; 1 Sam 8:11-18; 1 Kings 21:1-19.)

INDIVIDUAL LIBERTY (Freedom)

Liberty is gift from God to be exercised within His laws. Basic law of liberty is Ten Commandments, Mt 22 37-40, and to be conscientious toward God. (Ex 20:2; John 8:36, Acts 24:16; Gal 5:13; 1 Pet 2:16.)

LICENSE

Liberty licensed by majority, minority must conform. "Broad public policy" is "god," constitutional guarantees give way to consensus and "divine right" of public officials. (2 Pet 2:17-19; Jude 4,5; Rev 17&18).

STEWARDSHIP (Free Enterprise)

God created man to glorify Him & to tend His earth. Man is God's steward, to be fruitful, to fulfill God's dominion charter and to obey His work rules (Gen 1:18; 3; Lev 27:30-33; Dt 25.4; Mt 6:21,33; 25.14-20; Eph 6:5-9.)

COLLECTIVISM (Socialism)

Materialism is worshipped. Govt controls production & distribution. Man must serve State, not God. Property a privilege conferred or cancelled by State (Lk 12:13-21; Rev 13:16-17.)

Bible Reading Schedule

Those who want to be mature prayer warriors should read the Bible through once a year. In order to do this, one must cover three chapters on each weekday and five on Sunday. Years ago I heard of the following system which has served me and many others well ever since.

Very simply, the plan divides the Bible into six sections which I read on six weekdays. Monday's reading is from the Pentateuch (Genesis to Deuteronomy), Tuesday's from the historical books (Joshua to Esther), Wednesday's from the poetic books (Job to Song of Solomon), Thursday's from the prophets (Isaiah to Malachi), Friday's from the Gospels (Matthew to John), and Saturday's from the rest of the New Testament.

The schedule works like this: each day at least three chapters are read from the assigned section, the stopping place marked by a penciled date at the end of the passage. For example, if we read Genesis 1-3 on Monday, we mark the date at the end of chapter 3. Then the following Monday we erase last week's date and begin reading at chapter 4.

The same procedure will be followed on Joshua on Tuesday, Job on Wednesday, etc. The advantages of the date markings are many, including a gentle rebuke for negligence when the date is two or three weeks old!

Mercifully, the human mind cannot think two thoughts at once. When oppressive thoughts come, we are to displace them with appropriate scripture verses (II Corinthians 10:3-5). Even if we must repeat these verses many, many times, it is surely worth the effort in order to be completely free.

Daily Bible reading is actually *food for the spirit*. A memorized verse each day may be considered the spiritual "vitamin pill." Prayer in accordance with the will of God is based on Scripture. Therefore some pattern of daily reading of the Word is essential for the committed prayer warrior.

A CHAIN OF PRAYER

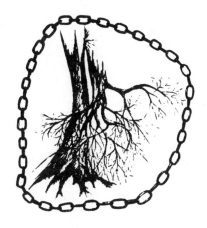

Do you ever wonder why God's people are often battered by earth's bully? Would you like to see the tide turned, for those that are in defeat? Why not be more than conquerors through Him who loved us and washed us from our sins in His own Blood?

Recently God reminded me of something He had shown me years ago. Once while in prayer, with my eyes closed, I saw a garden with the ugliest tree imaginable right in the center of it. As I watched, the tree was violently broken off by an unseen hand. Then the root was removed, and the scene changed. Next I saw mountains flying underneath, far faster than they would from an airplane. What did it mean?

"And *now* also the axe is laid unto the root of the trees: every tree therefore which bringeth not forth good fruit is hewn down, and cast into the fire." (Luke 3:9)

" . . . Wickedness shall be broken as a tree."
(Job 24:20)

Could it be that God is getting ready to remove the very root of evil from this planet? If so, do we have any part to play in this thrilling venture?

Remember the Lord's parable on prayer in Luke 18. It teaches that we should "pray and not faint." But the great point is, keep on praying *what*?

The widow asked, "Avenge me of mine adversary." How about us? If we ask for *this,* what shall we get?

The Lord Jesus Himself answered that question: "And shall not God *avenge* His own elect, *which cry day and night unto Him,* though He bear long with them? I tell you that He will *avenge* them *speedily.* Nevertheless when the Son of man cometh, shall He find faith on the earth?"

The italics point to God's purpose *now* as He prepares the world for the return of His Son. He will break off Satan's work and remove the devil from the face of the earth.

"And I saw an angel come down from heaven, having the key of the bottomless pit and *a great chain in his hand.* And he laid hold on the dragon, that old serpent, which is the devil and Satan, and bound him a thousand years . . . " (Rev. 20:1,2)

When God sends that angel to do the job, what kind of chain do you think He will use? How about a chain of prayer!

Some have already captured this vision and are organizing for 'round-the-clock' prayer. The 24 hours are divided into 48 half-hour segments. Believers sign up for the half hour they are most likely to be able to spend *every* day in prayer, putting their phone number on the sheet. One person serves as chairman, passing on urgent requests to the chain as they come. Some groups just use a simple, call-the-person-after-you method. Others have calling captains in each three-hour segment of time. Here are some guidelines for the actual praying;

1. *Praise* and *thank* the Father for Himself first; for His beloved Son, our Lord Jesus Christ, and His shed blood on our behalf; and for His Holy Spirit who empowers us. (Psalm 100:4)

2. Confess your sins and forgive anyone you have resented. (I John 1:9; Matt. 6:12, 14, 15)

3. Ask God to direct your prayer and protect you and your family with His holy angels.

4. Pray for each member of your local prayer chain by name, and lift their families and needs to the Lord. Those who pray must be covered by prayer themselves. Satan also knows what John Wesley knew: "God does nothing apart from prayer."

5. Pray for every pastor and priest in your city, that the Holy Spirit will come upon them in their pulpits and ministries, *this week.*

6. Pray, *"Avenge me, avenge us,* Thy people, of our adversary. Father, *remove* all satanism, occultism, witchcraft, astrology, heresy, freemasonry, and phony religion from the face of the earth. *Remove* blasphemy, pornography, crime, violence, immorality, alcoholism, drug addiction, communism, and greed from earth, in the Name of Jesus Christ.

7. *Bind* the evil spirits that would hinder the will of God for your family and the family of God in your area today, in the Name of Jesus Christ. (Matt. 18: 18-20; Matt. 12:29)

8. Pray for the Lord's soon return. Yes, this is

scriptural. In Revelation 22:7 the Lord promised, "Behold, I come quickly." In verse 20 the apostle John prayed, "Even so, come, Lord Jesus."

Is this prayer necessary? Consider. God told Jeremiah the Babylonian Captivity would last 70 years. Yet, when the time was up, Daniel fasted and prayed when he discovered that promise. Study Daniel 9 for victory prayer in crisis times.

"Pray without ceasing!" (I Thess. 5:17)

—Pat Brooks

THE WESTMINSTER SHORTER CATECHISM

1. What is the chief end of man?

Man's chief end is to glorify God , and to enjoy Him forever.

2. What rule hath God given to direct us how we may glorify and enjoy Him?

The word of God, which is contained in the Scriptures of the Old and New Testaments, is the only rule to direct us how we may glorify and enjoy Him.

3. What do the Scriptures principally teach?

The Scriptures principally teach, what man is to believe concerning God, and what duty God requires of man.

4. What is God?

God is a Spirit, infinite, eternal, and unchangeable, in His being, wisdom, power, holiness, justice, goodness, and truth.

5. Are there more gods than one?

There is but one only, the living and true God.

6. How many persons are there in the Godhead?

There are three persons in the Godhead, the Father, the Son, and the Holy Ghost; and these three are one God, the same in substance, equal in power and glory.

7. What are the decrees of God?

The decrees of God are, his eternal purpose, according to the counsel of his will, whereby, for his own glory, he hath foreordained whatsoever comes to pass.

8. How doth God execute his decrees?

God executeth his decrees in the works of creation and providence.

9. What is the work of creation?

The work of creation is, God's making all things of nothing, by the word of his power, in the space of six days, and all very good.

10. How did God create man?

God created man male and female, after his own image, in knowledge, righteousness, and holiness, with dominion over the creatures.

11. What are God's works of providence?

God's works of providence are, his most holy, wise, and powerful preserving and governing all his creatures, and all their actions.

12. What special act of providence did God exercise toward man in the estate wherein he was created?

When God had created man, he entered into a covenant of life with him, upon condition of perfect obedience; forbidding him to eat of the tree of the knowledge of good and evil, upon the pain of death.

13. Did our first parents continue\in the estate wherein they were created?

Our first parents, being left to the freedom of their own will, fell from the estate wherein they were created, by sinning against God.

14. What is sin?

Sin is any want of conformity unto, or transgression of, the law of God.

15. What was the sin whereby our first parents fell from the estate wherein they were created?

The sin whereby our first parents fell from the estate wherein they were created, was their eating the forbidden fruit.

16. Did all mankind fall in Adam's first transgression?

The covenant being made with Adam, not only for himself, but for his posterity; all mankind, descending from him by ordinary generation, sinned in him, and fell with him, in his first transgression.

17. Into what estate did the fall bring mankind?

The fall brought mankind into an estate of sin and misery.

18. Wherein consists the sinfulness of that estate whereinto man fell?

The sinfulness of that estate whereinto man fell, consists in the guilt of Adam's first sin, the want of original righteousness, and the corruption of his whole nature, which is commonly called Original Sin; together with all actual transgressions which proceed from it.

19. What is the misery of that estate whereinto man fell?

All mankind by their fall lost communion with God, are under his wrath and curse, and so made liable to all miseries in this life, to death itself, and the pains of hell for ever.

20. Did God leave all mankind to perish in the estate of sin and misery?

God having, out of his mere good pleasure, from all eternity, elected some to everlasting life, did enter into a covenant of grace, to deliver them out of the estate of sin and misery, and to bring them into an estate of salvation by a Redeemer.

21. Who is the Redeemer of God's elect?

The only Redeemer of God's elect is the Lord Jesus Christ, who, being the eternal Son of God, became man, and so was, and continueth to be, God and man in two distinct natures, and one person, for ever.

22. How did Christ, being the Son of God, become man?

Christ, the Son of God, became man, by taking to himself a true body, and a reasonable soul, being conceived by the power of the Holy Ghost, in the womb of the Virgin Mary, and born of her, yet without sin.

23. What offices doth Christ execute as our Redeemer?

Christ, as our Redeemer, executeth the offices of prophet, of a priest, and a king, both in his estate of humiliation and exaltation.

24. How doth Christ execute the office of a prophet?

Christ executeth the office of a prophet, in revealing to us, by his word and Spirit, the will of God for our salvation.

25. How doth Christ execute the office of a priest?

Christ executeth the office of a priest, in his once offering up of himself a sacrifice to satisfy divine justice, and reconcile us to God; and in making continual intercession for us.

26. How doth Christ execute the office of a king?

Christ executeth the office of a king, in subduing us to himself, in ruling and defending us, and in restraining and conquering all his and our enemies.

27. Wherein did Christ's humiliation consist?

Christ's humiliation consisted in his being born, and that in a low condition, made under the law, undergoing the miseries of this life, the wrath of God, and the cursed death of the cross; in being buried, and continuing under the power of death for a time.

28. Wherein consisteth Christ's exaltation?

Christ's exaltation consisteth in his rising again from the dead on the third day, in ascending up into heaven, in sitting at the right hand of God the Father, and in coming to judge the world at the last day.

29. How are we made partakers of the redemption purchased by Christ?

We are made partakers of the redemption purchased by Christ, by the effectual application of it to us by his Holy Spirit.

30. How doth the Spirit apply to us the redemption purchased by Christ?

The Spirit applieth to us the redemption purchased by Christ, by working faith in us, and thereby uniting us to Christ in our effectual calling.

31. What is effectual calling?

Effectual calling is the work of God's Spirit, whereby, convincing us of our sin and misery, enlightening our minds in the knowledge of Christ, and renewing our wills, He doth persuade and enable us to embrace Jesus Christ, freely offered to us in the gospel.

32. What benefits do they that are effectually called partake of in this life?

They that are effectually called do in this life partake of justification, adoption, sanctification, and the several benefits which, in this life, do either accompany or flow from them.

33. What is justification?

Justification is an act of God's free grace, wherein He pardoneth all our sins, and accepteth us as righteous in His sight, only for the righteousness of Christ, imputed to us, and received by faith alone.

34. What is adoption?

Adoption is an act of God's free grace whereby we are received into the number, and have a right to all the privileges, of the sons of God.

35. What is sanctification?

Sanctification is the work of God's free grace, whereby we are renewed in the whole man after the image of God, and are enabled more and more to die unto sin, and live unto righteousness.

36. What are the benefits which in this life do accompany or flow from justification, adoption, and sanctification?

The benefits which in this life do accompany or flow from justification, adoption, and sanctification, are: assurance of God's love, peace of conscience, joy in the Holy Ghost, increase of grace, and perseverance therein to the end.

37. What benefits do believers receive from Christ at death?

The souls of believers are at their death made perfect in holiness, and do immediately pass into glory; and their bodies, being still united to Christ, do rest in their graves until the resurrection.

38. What benefits do believers receive from Christ at the resurrection?

At the resurrection, believers, being raised up in glory, shall be openly acknowledged and acquitted in the day of judgment, and made perfectly blessed in the full enjoying of God to all eternity.

39. What is the duty which God requireth of man?

The duty which God requireth of man is obedience to His revealed will.

40. What did God at first reveal to man for the rule of his obedience?

The rule which God at first revealed to man for his obedience was the moral law.

41. Wherein is the moral law summarily comprehended?

The moral law is summarily comprehended in the ten commandments.

42. What is the sum of the ten commandments?

The sum of the ten commandments is, to love the Lord our God, with all our heart, with all our soul, with all our strength, and with all our mind; and our neighbor as ourselves.

43. What is the preface to the ten commandments?

The preface to the ten commandments is in these words, "I am the Lord thy God, which have brought thee out of the land of Egypt, out of the house of bondage."

44. What doth the preface to the ten commandments teach us?

The preface to the ten commandments teacheth us, that because God is the Lord, and our God, and Redeemer, therefore we are bound to keep all His commandments.

45. Which is the first commandment?

The first commandment is, "Thou shalt have no other gods before me."

46. What is required in the first commandment?

The first commandment requireth us to know and acknowledge God to be the only true God, and our God, and to worship and glorify Him accordingly.

47. What is forbidden in the first commandment?

The first commandment forbiddeth the denying, or not worshipping and glorifying, the true God, as God, and our God; and the giving the worship and glory to any other, which is due to Him alone.

48. What are we especially taught by these words, "before me," in the first commandment?

These words, "before me," in the first commandment, teach us that God, who seeth all things, taketh notice of, and is much displeased with, the sin of having any other god.

49. Which is the second commandment?

The second commandment is, "Thou shalt not make unto thee any graven image, or any likeness of any thing that is in heaven above, or that is in the earth beneath, or that is in the water under the earth: thou shalt not bow down thyself to them, nor serve them: for I the Lord thy God am a jealous God, visiting the iniquity of the fathers upon the children unto the third and fourth generation of them that hate me; and showing mercy unto thousands of them that love me, and keep my commandments."

50. What is required in the second commandment?

The second commandment requireth the receiving, observing, and deeping pure and entire, all such religious worship and ordinances as God hath appointed in His word.

51. What is forbidden in the second commandment?

The second commandment forbiddeth the worshipping of God by images, of any other way not appointed in His word.

52. What are the reasons annexed to the second commandment?

The reasons annexed to the second commandment are: God's sovereignty over us, His propriety in us, and the zeal He hath to His own worship.

53. Which is the third commandment?

The third commandment is, "Thou shalt not take the name of the Lord thy God in vain; for the Lord will not hold him guiltless that taketh his name in vain."

54. What is required in the third commandment?

The third commandment requireth the holy and reverent use of God's names, titles, attributes, ordinances, word, and works.

55. What is forbidden in the third commandment?

The third commandment forbiddeth all profaning of abusing of anything whereby God maketh Himself known.

56. What is the reason annexed to the third commandment?

The reason annexed to the third commandment is, that however the breakers of this commandment may escape punishment from men, yet the Lord our God will not suffer them to escape His righteous judgment.

57. Which is the fourth commandment?

The fourth commandment is, " Remember the sabbath day, to keep it holy. Six days shalt thou labour, and do all thy work: but the seventh day is the sabbath of the Lord thy God: in it thou shalt not do any work, thou, nor thy son, nor thy daughter, thy manservant, nor thy maidservant, nor thy cattle, nor thy stranger that is within thy gates: for in six days the Lord made heaven and earth, the sea, and all that in them is, and rested the seventh day: wherefore the Lord blessed the sabbath day, and hallowed it."

58. What is required in the fourth commandment?

The fourth commandment requireth the keeping holy to God such set times as He hath appointed in His word; expressly one whole day in seven, to be a holy Sabbath to Himself.

59. Which day of the seven hath God appointed to be the weekly Sabbath?

From the beginning of the world to the resurrection of Christ, God appointed the seventh day to the week to be the weekly Sabbath; and the first day of the week, ever since, to continue to the end of the world, which is the Christian Sabbath.

60. How is the Sabbath to be sanctified?

The Sabbath is to be sanctified by a holy resting all that day, even from such worldly employments and recreations as are lawful on other days; and spending the whole time in the public and private exercises of God's worship, except so much as is to be taken up in the works of necessity and mercy.

61. What is forbidden in the fourth commandment?

The fourth commandment forbiddeth the omission, or careless performance, of the duties required, and the profaning the day by idleness, or doing that which is in itself sinful, or by unnecessary thoughts, words, or works, about our worldly employments or recreations.

62. What are the reasons annexed to the fourth commandment?

The reasons annexed to the fourth commandment are, God's allowing us six days of the week for our own employments, His challenging a special propriety in the seventh, His own example, and His blessing the Sabbath day.

63. Which is the fifth commandment?

The fifth commandment is, "Honor thy father and thy mother; that thy days may be long upon the land which the Lord thy God giveth thee."

64. What is required in the fifth commandment?

The fifth commandment requireth the preserving the honor, and performing the duties, belong to everyone in their several places and relations, as superiors, inferiors, or equals.

65. What is forbidden in the fifth commandment?

The fifth commandment forbiddeth the neglecting of, or doing anything against the honor and duty which belongeth to everyone in their several places and relations.

66. What is the reason annexed to the fifth commandment?

The reason annexed to the fifth commandment is, a promise of long life and prosperity (as far as it shall serve for God's glory, and their own good) to all such as keep this commandment.

67. Which is the sixth commandment?

The sixth commandment is, "Thou shalt not kill."

68. What is required in the sixth commandment?

The sixth commandment requireth all lawful endeavors to preserve our own life, and the life of others.

69. What is forbidden in the sixth commandment?

The sixth commandment forbiddeth the taking away of our own life, or the life of our neighbor unjustly, or whatsoever tendeth thereunto.

70. Which is the seventh commandment?

The seventh commandment is, "Thou shalt not commit adultery."

71. What is required in the seventh commandment?

The seventh commandment requireth the preservation of our own and our neighbor's chastity, in heart, speech, and behavior.

72. What is forbidden in the seventh commandment?

The seventh commandment forbiddeth at unchaste thoughts, words, and actions.

73. Which is the eighth commandment?

The eighth commandment is, "Thou shalt not steal."

74. What is required in the eighth commandment?

The eighth commandment requireth the lawful procuring and furthering the wealth and outward estate of ourselves and others.

75. What is forbidden in the eighth commandment?

The eighth commandment forbiddeth whatsoever doth, or may, unjustly hinder our own or our neighbor's wealth or outward estate.

76. Which is the ninth commandment?

The ninth commandment is, "Thou shalt not bear false witness against thy neighbor."

77. What is required in the ninth commandment?

The ninth commandment requireth the maintaining and promoting of truth between man and man, and of our own and our neighbor's good name, especially in witness-bearing.

78. What is forbidden in the ninth commandment?

The ninth commandment forbiddeth whatsoever is prejudicial to truth, or injurious to our own or our neighbor's good name.

79. Which is the tenth commandment?

The tenth commandment is, "Thou shalt not covet thy neighbor's house, thou shalt not covet thy neighbor's wife, no his manservant, nor his maidservant, nor his ox, nor his ass, nor any thing that is thy neighbor's."

80. What is required in the tenth commandment?

The tenth commandment requireth full contentment with our own condition, with a right and charitable frame of spirit toward our neighbor, and all that is his.

81. What is forbidden in the tenth commandment?

The tenth commandment forbiddeth all discontentment with our own estate, envying or grieving at the good of our neighbor, and all inordinate motions and affections to anything that is his.

82. Is any man able perfectly to keep the commandments of God?

No mere man, since the fall, is able, in this life, perfectly to keep the commandments of God; but doth daily break them, in thought, word, and deed.

83. Are all transgression of the law equally heinous?

Some sins in themselves, and by reason of several aggravations, are more heinous in the sight of God than others.

84. What doth every sin deserve?

Every sin deserveth God's wrath and curse, both in this life, and that which is to come.

85. What doth God require of us, that we may escape His wrath and curse, due to us for sin?

To escape the wrath and curse of God, due to us for sin, God requireth of us faith in Jesus Christ, repentance unto life, with the diligent use of all the outward means whereby Christ communicateth to us the benefits of redemption.

86. What is faith in Jesus Christ?

Faith in Jesus Christ is a saving grace, whereby we receive and rest upon Him alone for salvation, as He is offered to us in the gospel.

87. What is repentance unto life?

Repentance unto life is a saving grace, whereby a sinner, out of a true sense of his sin, and apprehension of the mercy of God in Christ, doth, with grief and hatred of his sin, turn from it unto God, with full purpose of, and endeavor after, new obedience.

88. What are the outward and ordinary means whereby Christ communicateth to us the benefits of redemption?

The outward and ordinary means whereby Christ communicateth to us the benefits of redemption are, His ordinances, especially the word, sacraments, and prayer; all of which are made effectual to the elect for salvation.

89. How is the word made effectual to salvation?

The Spirit of God maketh the reading, but especially the preaching, of the word, an effectual means of convincing and converting sinners, and of building them up in holiness and comfort through faith unto salvation.

90. How is the word to be read and heard, that it may become effectual to salvation?

That the word may become effectual to salvation, we must attend thereunto with diligence, preparation, and prayer; receive it with faith and love, lay it up in our hearts, and practice it in our lives.

91. How do the sacraments become effectual means of salvation?

The sacraments become effectual means of salvation, not from any virtue in them, or in him that doth administer them; but only by the blessing of Christ, and the working of His Spirit in them that by faith receive them.

92. What is a sacrament?

A sacrament is a holy ordinance instituted by Christ, wherein, by sensible signs, Christ and the benefits of the new covenant are represented, sealed and applied to believers.

93. Which are the sacraments of the New Testament?

The sacraments of the New Testament are, baptism, and the Lord's supper.

94. What is baptism?

Baptism is a sacrament, wherein the washing with water, in the name of the Father, and the Son, and of the Holy Ghost, doth

181

signify and seal our ingrafting into Christ, and partaking of the benefits of the covenant of grace, and our engagement to be the Lord's.

95. To whom is baptism to be administered?

Baptism is not to be administered to any that are out of the visible church, till they profess their faith in Christ, and obedience to Him; but the infants of such as are members of the visible church, are to be baptized.

96. What is the Lord's supper?

The Lord's supper is a sacrament, wherein, by giving and receiving bread and wine, according to Christ's appointment, His death is showed forth; and the worthy receivers are, not after a corporal and carnal manner, but by faith, made partakers of His body and blood, with all His benefits, to their spiritual nourishment and growth in grace.

97. What is required to the worthy receiving of the Lord's supper?

It is required of them that would that they examine themselves, of their knowledge to discern the Lord's body, of their faith to feed upon Him, of their repentance, love, and new obedience; lest coming unworthily, they eat and drink judgment to themselves.

98. What is prayer?

Prayer is an offering up of our desires unto God, for things agreeable to His will, in the name of Christ, with confession of our sins, and thankful acknowledgment of His mercies.

99. What rule hath God given for our direction in prayer?

The whole word of God is of use to direct us in prayer; but the special rule of direction is that form of prayer, which Christ taught His disciples, commonly called, "The Lord's prayer."

100. What doth the preface of the Lord's prayer teach us?

The preface of the Lord's prayer, which is, "Our Father which art in heaven," teacheth us to draw near to God, with all holy reverence and confidence, as children to a father, able and ready to help us; and that we should pray with and for others.

101. What do we pray for in the first petition?

In the first petition, which is, "Hallowed by thy name," we pray, that God would enable us, and others, to glorify Him in all that whereby He maketh Himself known, and that He would dispose all things to His own glory.

102. What do we pray for in the second petition?

In the second petition, which is, "Thy kingdom come," we pray, that Satan's kingdom may be destroyed, and that the kingdom of grace may be advanced, ourselves and others brought into it, and kept in it, and that the kingdom of glory may be hastened.

103. What do we pray for in the third petition?

In the third petition, which is, "Thy will be done in earth, as it is in heaven," we pray, that God, by His grace, would make us able and willing to know, obey, and submit to His will in all things as the angels do in heaven.

104. What do we pray for in the fourth petition?

In the fourth petition, which is, "Give us this day our daily bread," we pray, that, of God's free gift, we may receive a competent portion of the good things of this life, and enjoy His blessing with them.

105. What do we pray for in the fifth petition?

In the fifth petition, which is, "And forgive us our debts, as we forgive our debtors," we pray, that God, for Christ's sake, would freely pardon all our sins; which we are the rather encouraged to ask, because by His grace we are enabled from the heart to forgive others.

106. What do we pray for in the sixth petition?

In the sixth petition, which is, "And lead us not into temptation, but deliver us from evil," We pray that God would either keep us from being tempted to sin, or support and deliver us when we are tempted.

107. What doth the conclusion of the Lord's prayer teach us?

The conclusion of the Lord's prayer, which is, "For thine is the kingdom, and the power, and the glory, for ever, Amen," teacheth us to take our encouragement in prayer from God only, and in our prayers to praise Him, ascribing kingdom, power, and glory to Him, and in testimony of our desire and assurance to be heard, we say, Amen.

Quantity Prices: *Freedom — or Slavery?*

1 copy: $7 postpaid
2 copies: $12 postpaid
4 copies: $20 postpaid
10 copies: $40 postpaid
Box: 60% off, plus shipping; phone for details

Please order from the source nearest you:

New Puritan Library
91 Lytle Road
Fletcher, NC 28732
(704) 628-2185

New Puritan Library
P.O. Box 247
Walnut Creek, CA 94596
(415) 934-7019

Emissary Publications
9205 SE Clackamas Road
Clackamas, OR 97015
(503) 824-2050

Books by Pat Brooks

Healing of the Mind, This dynamic bestseller (55,000 now in print) has kept some from suicide. Reveals God's answer to your problems with self-life and demonic torment. 4-1/4 x 7, 151 pp. **$2.50**

Daughters of the King, Pat Brooks' uplifting, incisive book on the woman's role. 2nd edition has Study Guide for Bible teachers, classes. 5-3/8 x 8, 160 pp. **$5**

For Parents and Patriots: Pat Brooks' classic, **Return of the Puritans,** new 5th edition, dynamites apathy! Last 4 chapters updated with Oliver North, the NEA war on Christian schools, and the AIDS plague. 5-3/8 x 8, 190 pp. **$5**

Other Powerful NPL Books

Ten Commandments for Now, by Stephen Crotts, is a winner! Readable and relevant, it pulls no punches. Either return to God's laws, or be broken by them! Youths "whys" answered here. 4-1/4 x 7, 100+ pp. **$2.50**

Moments With Martha, Martha Ferrin, popular radio personality and Bible teacher, shares 5 common Christian "crimes" and their cures. Delightful book! 4-1/4 x 7, 128 pp. **$2.50**

10 TITLES FOR $10.00
(Plus $2 shipping)

Rapture? Condensed version of Dave MacPherson's GREAT RAPTURE HOAX: quick reading with much meat. Has 21 pages of quotes from church leaders over 2,000 years — all Post-Trib! 5-3/8 x 8, 71 pp.**$2.50**

For Lower Primary Grades, **The Pilgrim Primer,** by Jan Payne Pierce, a favorite with Christian schools, home schoolers. Tells story of Mayflower crossing and *Compact:* First Thanksgiving. 5-3/8 x 8, 26 pp.   **$1.50**

For Mid-Primary Grades: **The Puritan Primer,** Pierce's magnificent history of the "Bible State." Let your children find out why the Reds hate the Puritans! 5-3/8 x 8, 37 pp.**$1.50**

For Middle School: **The Patriot Primer,** Jan Pierce's masterpiece. The **Declaration** & War for Independence; birth of the republic. Everything from George Washington to Oliver North! 5-3/8 x 8, 81 pp.   **$2.50**

Not Healed? Charlotte Collins' comforting narrative of God's faithfulness when her husband died of cancer. For the bereaved. 4-1/4 x 7, 126 pp.   **$2.50**

John 8:32 Packet!
5 Books for $18 Postpaid

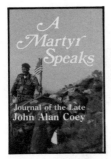

A Martyr Speaks, Journal of an American soldier killed in Rhodesia in 1975 defending Christian freedom. "Great literature: spiritually uplifting; morally and politically discerning; emotionally cleansing and moving . . . a superb role model and hero for a generation that has few." 246 pp.　　　　　　**$7**

Should a Christian Be a Mason? E.M. Storms removes the veil from freemasonry in this documented research work, using authoritative books of famous Masons. Rev. Jim Shaw, former 33rd degree Mason, has foreword, lecture on the 32nd degree. 4-1/4 x 7, 110 pp.　　　　　　**$2.50**

The Budding Fig Tree, by Roy R. Newman & Pat Brooks. Pure dynamite: the Israel issue; Post-Tribulation eschatology; even a page from the *Apocalypse of Peter* (first-century work early Christians had). 5-3/8 x 8, 66 pp.　　　　　　**$2.50**

A Call to War/Prayer Power (2 books in one) for mature believers. Red control of the West; spiritual warfare to counter; fasting; prayer; giving. 5-3/8 x 8, 224 pp.　　　　**$7**

The Six-Pointed Star, by Dr. O.J. Graham. A Christian author of Jewish heritage exposes the hexagram as the most evil of all occult symbols. Superb documentation. 4-1/4 x 7, 122 pp.　　　　　　**$2.50**